Straight Talk About Prejudice

Rachel Kranz

☑ Facts On File

Straight Talk About Prejudice

Facts On File, Inc.
460 Park Avenue South
New York NY 10016
USA

Library of Congress Cataloging-in-Publication Data
Kranz, Rachel.
 Straight talk about prejudice / by Rachel Kranz.
  p. cm.
 Includes bibliographical references and index.
 Summary: Discusses the causes and effects of prejudice and stereotyping and how such thinking can lead to discrimination against such groups as women, ethnic groups, homosexuals, the aging, and the handicapped.
 ISBN 0-8160-2488-X
 1. Toleration—Juvenile literature. 2. Prejudices—Juvenile literature. 3. Discrimination—Juvenile literature. [1. Prejudices. 2. Discrimination.] I. Title.
HM276.K73 1992
303.3'85—dc20   91-3720

A British CIP catalogue record for this book is available from the British Library.

Facts On File books are available at special discounts when purchased in bulk quantities for businesses, associations, institutions or sales promotions. Please call our Special Sales Department in New York at 212/683-2244 (dial 800/322-8755 except in NY, AK or HI) or in Oxford at 865/728399.

Text design by Catherine Hyman
Jacket design by Catherine Hyman
Composition by Facts On File, Inc.
Manufactured by the Maple-Vail Book Manufacturing Group
Printed in the United States of America

10 9 8 7 6 5 4 3 2

This book is printed on acid-free paper.

Contents

1. About Prejudice   1

2. Racial and Cultural Prejudice   25

3. Prejudice Against Women   58

4. Prejudice Against Homosexuals   76

5. Prejudice Against the Aged and the Handicapped   94

6. Coping with Prejudice   106

7. Where to Find Help   109

Index   121

1

About Prejudice

Prejudice, Discrimination, and Stereotypes

The word *prejudice* comes from two Latin words that are also the basis of the word *prejudge*. To have prejudice against a person or a group is to *prejudge* him, her, or it, to think that you already know everything about that person or that group, just on the basis of one or two facts. If a person thinks that women are not good drivers, or that people of a particular race are likely to be lazy or poorly educated, that person is *prejudiced*. He or she is prejudging a person, simply on the basis of being a woman or being of a particular racial group.

If that's our definition, then who is "prejudiced" and who is not? As you might imagine, in some ways, we are all prejudiced. It's impossible to go through life without making some assumptions about people, right or wrong. If you heard a story about a woman athlete, you would probably have good reason for assuming that she wasn't a professional football player. If you knew that a certain neighborhood was mainly Irish, or mainly Italian, you might have some reason to assume that your Jewish friend didn't live there. Of course, in either case, you might be wrong. Your *prejudices*, or assumptions about people, might turn out to be contradicted by the facts.

At this point, some of you may be thinking, well, if it's impossible not to be prejudiced, then what's so bad about it? And if everybody is prejudiced, doesn't it all balance out in the end?

If prejudice were just a matter of thinking and holding opinions, it wouldn't be such a big problem. Unfortunately, it goes further than that. Prejudice leads to *discrimination*: preventing some people from having rights or benefits that other people enjoy, simply on the basis of what group they belong to. When some people are paid less than others for doing the same job, or when some people are not allowed to do a certain job even though they are qualified for it, that's discrimination.

There are many other examples of discrimination. People may be discriminated against in housing (not being allowed to live in certain buildings or certain neighborhoods), in education (not being allowed to get certain training or attend certain schools), in politics (not being elected or appointed to office because of the group they belong to), and generally in society (not being allowed into a restaurant or other public place; being asked to ride in special train cars or special parts of a bus; being served last in a store or government office).

Sometimes discrimination is legal. In some parts of the United States, for example, there used to be laws against African Americans and white people marrying each other. In other places, the law allowed people to sell their houses with certain "restrictions": If you wanted to buy a "restricted" home, you had to promise that you would not resell the house to someone who was Jewish. Until the middle of the 19th century, African Americans did not have the legal right to vote; until the early part of the 20th century, women did not have that right, either. American Indians gained the right to vote when they were made U.S. citizens in 1924, but even so, as with African Americans, several more decades of legislation and activism were required to make that right a reality.

Sometimes, discrimination is a matter of organized practice. Many graduate schools, for example, used to have "quotas," or limits, on the number of Jews they would accept. This was not a matter of law. It was not even a public matter. But the people who made the decisions about who could enter the school were organized to practice discrimination. Likewise, it used to be very difficult for women to get into law school or medical school. Many people held the prejudice, or assumption, that women would never finish their education or would get married, have children, and quit their professions soon after they graduated, so that it was not worthwhile to educate them.

Sometimes discrimination is more subtle. A store owner who does not wait on someone of a certain race or who makes it clear that homeless people are "not welcome" even if they are doing nothing wrong, is practicing discrimination. The store owner may not even realize that she or he is prejudiced or notice the discriminatory behavior. The person's assumptions may simply seem like reality. If asked, he or she might say, "But those people all steal—I have to keep them out of my store." The store owner might be prejudiced without even knowing it.

Often, people's prejudices take the form of *stereotypes.* A stereotype is an assumption about how a whole group of people will behave. It is a convenient image that seems to be real, but is really only a large, prejudiced assumption.

One common stereotype is that of the "crazy woman driver." This is an image that everyone is familiar with. We can all remember many television shows or movies in which a bewildered woman doesn't know how to put her car into reverse or rams into another person's car because she is so silly and inept.

If this image seems familiar to us, we may unconsciously believe that it is actually true. Without our even realizing it, this stereotype may affect the way we think about women and their ability to drive. Both women and men may be affected by this stereotype. Both may believe that "most women are not very good drivers," or "generally, in an emergency, I'd rather have a man at the wheel."

The funny thing about stereotypes is that they're so hard to disprove. If a man has absorbed the stereotype about women drivers, for example, he will feel that this stereotype is confirmed every time he sees a woman driving badly. Likewise, if a woman has absorbed this stereotype, she may believe that most women drive badly, even if you point out to her that she herself drives quite well. "Yes, but *most* women . . ." she might object. Even if you point out to her that she knows 10 good women drivers for every bad one, or that she knows more bad men drivers than bad women drivers, she may still continue to believe that *most* women are bad drivers. Somehow, the stereotype continues to have power, even when it is proven not to be true.

Stereotypes in Your Life

Just as we are all affected by prejudice in some way, we are all affected by stereotypes. Sometimes stereotypes affect the way we see other people. Other times, they affect how others see us—or even how we see ourselves.

One major stereotype that probably affects you is the stereotype that many adults have about teenagers. Which of the following items do you recognize as part of a common stereotype of teenagers? What other items would you add to complete the stereotype?

Teenagers Are:

- irresponsible
- lazy
- poor students

- always listening to loud music
- always interested in sex
- sloppy dressers with messy hair
- rude, especially to adults
- on drugs
- dangerous drivers
- always having fun
- carefree, with nothing serious on their minds
- unconcerned about the future

Do any of these items seem generally true to you? Do any items seem true of other teenagers while not applying to *you*? Do any items seem to apply only to a small minority but not to most teenagers you know?

Thinking about the difference between the stereotype and the reality of teenagers helps show how stereotypes work. Of course, some of the items on the list above do apply to some teenagers—but they don't apply to every single teenager. Furthermore, every item on the list might also apply to some adults. Nevertheless, the stereotype remains powerful: Whenever a teenager has a quality on the list, it seems to confirm the truth of the stereotype, whereas any teenager who is different is the "exception." Likewise, an adult who dresses in a sloppy way, takes drugs, or drives dangerously does not weaken the stereotype. Instead of showing that the qualities on the list might belong to anybody, regardless of age, the adult might actually be told that he or she is "acting like a teenager!"

Furthermore, a stereotype suggests that anybody who has one stereotypical quality must have all the rest, as well. So, adults who see a teenager listening to loud music or dressed in torn jeans might assume that "he must be on drugs" or "she probably never thinks about her future." What do you think? Is there any relationship between how people dress and the kind of students they are or how responsible they are? Have you ever felt frustrated by the assumptions that someone was making about you?

One of the reasons people are so attracted to stereotypes is that they seem to hold so much useful information. If people have the stereotype of a teenager in mind, they may believe that they know everything they need to know about every teenager they meet. Likewise, people frequently have stereotypes about fat people, good students, "jocks," "wimps," attractive people, "ugly" people, people who wear leather jackets, people who dress "preppy," people with money, people without money, people who live in certain neighborhoods, and so on. The stereotypes about such people seem to hold a lot of information: fat people are probably "pathetic," "unattractive," "emotionally troubled"; good students must be "nerds," "too smart," "arrogant," "good at books but bad with people"; "jocks" are most likely "dumb," "clumsy," "only interested in sports," and so on. On the other hand, attractive people or popular kids may be stereotyped as "fun to be with," "nice," "interesting," "exciting," and other positive images.

Think about the people you want to go out with, be friends with, get to know, or avoid. To what extent do you use stereotypes to help you make these decisions? To what extent do you go by a first impression plus a stereotype that you believe tells you everything you need to know, positive or negative? To what extent do you believe people go by stereotypes about you, stereotypes that may not give them a true picture of who you really are?

Prejudice and History

So far, we've mainly been talking about stereotypes that could apply to just about any group of people. However, some stereotypes concern particular racial, cultural, or sexual groups. These stereotypes are also shaped by prejudice: the assumptions that people in one racial, cultural, or sexual group make about people in another.

One of the worst and most powerful aspects of prejudice is the way that it can seem "natural." Sometimes it may seem that black and white people just "naturally" do not get along, that white people have always looked down on people of color and have always discriminated against them. Or it may seem that Jews and Arabs, or Jews and Christians, have never been able to live side by side in peace. Stereotypes can make it seem as though "men are just like that" or "what else can you expect from women?" When a particular kind of prejudice runs very deep, sometimes it can seem as though the prejudice has always existed and will always exist, as though it were as much a fact of life as people's need to eat or to shelter themselves.

In fact, prejudice is not something "natural" and unchanging. Rather, it is something that people create, and therefore it is constantly changing—and something that we can work together to change.

Dark- and light-skinned people have not "always" been at odds, nor have "white" Europeans always looked down on darker-skinned people of other heritages. On the contrary, during the Middle Ages, Europeans considered the nations of Africa rich kingdoms full of fabulous golden cities whose culture and civilization were far superior to their own. Likewise, they looked up to the Asian peoples of India and China, whose manufactured goods, such as porcelain, cloth, utensils and ornaments were of much higher quality than anything that could be made in Europe.

In Spain's so-called Golden Age, from 950 to 1250, Jews, Christians, and Muslims lived side by side in harmony under the rule of the Moors. The Moors were dark-skinned Arabs who, though Muslim themselves, promoted religious and cultural tolerance. In fact, some places of worship were actually shared by all three religions, each of which had different holy days. This harmony continued past the Golden Age until 1492, when the new European Christian rulers, King Ferdinand and Queen Isabella, expelled both Moors and Jews from Spain and made Christianity the only official religion.

Sometimes a group that is the target of prejudice eventually manages to overcome stereotyping and discrimination. The Irish, for example, have had a long history as the objects of prejudice, both in their native Ireland and in the United States. In Ireland, they faced many laws made by the ruling British Empire, demanding that they speak English instead of their native Gaelic and preventing them from voting, holding political office, serving on juries, testifying against the British in court, or holding large meetings without permission.

When poverty and discrimination drove many Irish to emigrate to the United States in the mid-1800s, they found new types of discrimination and prejudice. They might expect to see many jobs in the want ads accompanied by the words *No Irish need apply*. Other Americans stereotyped them as criminals, so that the expression *paddywagon*—the police van that takes people under arrest to jail—got its name from *paddy*, a slang term for Irish. The largest mass lynching in U.S. history took place in the mid-1800s, when 10 Irish Americans were hanged.

Eventually, the Irish in America managed to overcome much of the prejudice against them. Ironically, the same stereotypes that had been directed against the Irish in the mid-1800s went on to haunt southern and central Europeans—Italians, Poles, Russians, and Lithuanians—who immigrated to America in the late 1800s. These ethnic groups were also stereotyped as "criminal," as well as lazy, irresponsible, childlike, and over-sexed. These very same stereotypes persist to this day—only now they are applied to African Americans and Hispanic Americans.

As you can see, some prejudices and stereotypes that once seemed "natural" and permanent now seem silly and hard to understand. The prejudices and stereotypes of our own time, however, are harder to overcome. Once again, that's partly because there may be some truth in them. Just as there may have been *some* Irish criminals or *some* lazy Italians, nowadays there may be *some* African Americans or Hispanic Americans to whom some parts of a stereotype may apply.

But once we know that we are dealing with stereotypes, not reality, we can look a little deeper to find the whole truth. And once we understand that prejudice is not fixed and natural, we can start to look for ways to overcome it.

It may also be helpful to remember that not all human societies are marked by prejudice. *Anthropologists* are people who study a wide range of societies in order to broaden our knowledge of human behavior. Anthropologists also study societies that existed in earlier times, before human beings could write and leave formal records. Many anthropologists believe that hunting and gathering societies, such as those of the native peoples of North America and Siberia, were without "prejudice" as we think of it. Although various tribes or nations might fight one another over territory and resources, these conflicts were not shaped by the idea that one group was superior to another.

Likewise, in the Roman Empire, a powerful empire centered in the Italian city of Rome from the 1st century B.C. through the 5th century A.D., many European and Asian peoples were conquered by the Romans, and many were made slaves. After a nation was conquered, however, its people were allowed to continue in their old way of life. If citizens of the conquered nation came to Rome, they did not face discrimination in housing, employment, or political activity. Certainly, skin color was not the basis of discrimination the way it has been in the United States.

Other kinds of prejudice that seem natural to us would not have seemed at all natural at other times in history. For example, many people today assume that homosexuality is unnatural, but in ancient Greece, homosexual relations between older men and younger men were considered as natural as male-female relationships. Many other cultures have varying attitudes toward homosexuality, from repression, to ignoring its existence, to tolerance.

Attitudes toward men and women have changed so much in the past few years that old prejudices exist side by side with new attitudes. In the 1950s, many experts insisted that mothers with jobs outside the home were virtually condemning their children to become juvenile delinquents. Today, working mothers are accepted to a far greater extent. In the 1900s, most people were prejudiced against the idea of women voting, whereas today it seems "natural" for women to vote and to hold political office. In fact, until a few decades ago, women wearing pants seemed scandalous, whereas today it is barely noticeable, even in formal or business circles. What assumptions and prejudices about men and women do we hold today that may look silly or "unnatural" in 20 or 30 or 50 years?

What Causes Prejudice?

If prejudice is not something natural and unchanging, then it must have causes—reasons why it springs up at a particular time and in a particular form. And the more we know about what causes prejudice, the better equipped we are to combat it.

Prejudice has many different causes that may work together, reinforcing one another. Sometimes it's hard to look at a situation and understand how and why people can be prejudiced—but if you look hard enough, you will find that there always is a reason.

Cultural Differences

Sometimes prejudice is simply the result of a lack of information. Every person grows up with particular ways of acting, ways that come partly from family, partly from culture or religion. These customs teach us ideas about right and wrong, polite and impolite, good and bad behavior.

Since every culture has its own ideas about these concepts, a person from one culture might easily misunderstand the behavior of a person from another. Some Asian societies, for example, believe that all adults in a community are responsible for disciplining children, whether they are members of the same family or not. Most European cultures, on the other hand, believe that only parents or other family members have the right to discipline a child. If an Asian-American storekeeper disciplines the unruly child of an Irish-American customer, the Irish parent may be shocked at the Asian's rudeness, while the Asian may be hurt and insulted at the parent's angry reaction. Each culture may end up prejudiced against the other ("They're so interfering!" "They don't even know how to discipline their own children!"), simply because of a lack of understanding.

Here is a list of areas where cultural standards vary widely. What are your own ideas about "right" and "wrong" in these cases? Are you aware of other standards that differ from your own? How might different standards lead to misunderstandings, prejudice, and stereotypes?

- table manners: Is it acceptable or not acceptable to eat with your fingers, burp after a meal, ask for seconds, refuse seconds, eat from a common plate, or comment on how you like your food?
- saying thank you: When do you say it and to whom? (In some cultures, it's an insult to say "thank you" to a friend or family member, because it implies that the person is a stranger who needs to be thanked, rather than someone who can be counted on without question.)
- children's behavior: Should they be "seen and not heard" or encouraged to express themselves? Should they be allowed to run around freely or supervised every minute? Can they be disciplined only by family members or also by other adults?
- being a host: Are you ever allowed to say "no" to a guest? Are you supposed to anticipate your guest's needs or wait until your guest asks for what he or she wants? Do you treat guests differently or the same as family members? (In some cultures, it's a mark of affection to tease guests and act as though they are "members of the

family"; in other cultures, this would be unspeakably rude.)

- being a guest: Is it rude to express a preference of your own or rude not to, especially if you are asked? Are you supposed to bring your host a thank-you present, or is this a rudeness implying that you think your host is poor or in need of help? Are you supposed to relax and make yourself "one of the family," or are you supposed to show at all times that you are aware of being a guest in someone else's home?

- male-female behavior: Is it rude for men to flirt and make admiring remarks to or about a woman—or is it more rude for them to ignore her? Are men supposed to show women certain courtesies, such as opening doors and holding coats, or do these actions imply that the man thinks the woman is weak and can't take care of herself? Is there certain language that men should not use in front of women? Are women supposed to serve men food and act as hostesses, or should they expect men to "help themselves"? If a woman assumes that she will pay her own way on a date, is she rudely implying that the man isn't capable of fulfilling his responsibilities?

As you can see, there is a wide variety of standards of behavior that govern almost every area of our lives. Most of our standards are so familiar that we aren't even aware of them—until someone else comes along and acts differently. If we're not aware that our way is not the only way, we may respond with prejudice or stereotypes, instead of seeing that different people simply do things differently.

Economic Competition

One situation in which prejudice is likely to occur is when one group of people feels that another is somehow threatening its livelihood. If members of a new ethnic group move into a city, for example, the original residents may worry that these newcomers will be willing to do the same jobs for less money. The newcomers may be perceived as "taking jobs away" from the people who were there first.

Sometimes economic competition and cultural misunderstandings work together to create intense prejudice. In the 19th and early 20th centuries, the mine owners of Minnesota's Iron Range employed members of many different ethnic groups: Irish, Poles, Finns, Scandinavians, Slavs, and several others. Employers would deliberately place members of different immigrant groups side by side in the mines, so that people could literally not speak to one another. The owners consciously created a climate of fear and suspicion, in which each group feared that the other would work for lower wages or take jobs away.

As you can imagine, this type of economic competition led to prejudice and stereotyping. Each group thought the other groups were lazy, greedy, deceitful, ignorant, and rude. Each group saw the others as its enemies in the fight for jobs and economic survival.

In that case, prejudice was overcome when the immigrants realized that they all had one goal in common: better wage and working conditions. They found ways to communicate across the language barrier and work together, rather than compete. They were able to form a trade union that included many different ethnic groups, with an agreement that no one group would make a separate deal with the employer; instead, they would all stick together. Because they could overcome their prejudices, they were able to work together to achieve a common goal.

Economic competition can involve issues other than jobs. It might concern government services or benefits, places in a graduate or professional school, or political positions. Any time that resources are scarce, people are scared of losing what they have. Rightly or wrongly, they may see other ethnic groups as taking away "their" jobs, services, places in school, or political offices.

Another economic issue that can foster prejudice is the question of property values—how much a person is able to get for selling or renting a house or apartment. Property values depend on many factors, including the neighborhood that a property is located in. If a neighborhood is seen as "desirable"—safe, clean, attractive—people are usually willing to pay more money to live there.

Thus, homeowners or landlords may fear that the presence of a new ethnic group will make property values go down. They think this for two reasons. On the one hand, stereotypes portray some ethnic groups as "dirty," "sloppy," "dangerous," or "criminal." According to the stereotype, if members of these groups move into a home or an apartment building, they will bring with them crime, drug dealers, and many other dangerous elements. Stereotypes also suggest that they may play loud music late at night, fail to discipline their children, neglect the upkeep of their property, and generally make the neighborhood or apartment building a less clean and pleasant place to live.

Even if none of the new residents behave in a way that fits this stereotype, the neighborhood's original residents may still worry about property values going down. They may feel that they just don't want to live near "those people," so they sell their homes, and move away. If just having people of a certain ethnic group in a neighborhood makes it less desirable to other groups, people of that neighborhood will find it more difficult to sell their homes. Thus, property values go down even if the new residents are just as clean and well behaved as the old ones.

In such an atmosphere, people may blame the new residents for the decline in property values, rather than correctly assigning responsibility to the prejudiced people who moved away or refused to move in. People whose entire lives have been spent paying for their homes may thus see members of other ethnic groups as an economic threat.

As you can see, the prejudice that results from economic competition may be a response to a real situation. Perhaps people really are facing unemployment, government cutbacks, or declining property values. However, instead of correctly understanding how these difficult situations were created, people turn to prejudice and stereotypes to explain the problem. Instead of blaming the employer who moves his or her factory to another state, people may blame another ethnic group for "taking away all the jobs." Instead of being angry at those who refuse to live in a diverse neighborhood, people may blame the ethnic newcomers who are also looking to improve their way of life. In order to overcome these types of prejudice, people have to find a different way of understanding economic competition and its causes.

Insecurity

Often, prejudice springs from insecurity—people's sense that they are being threatened by forces they don't completely understand and can't control.

We've seen how economic insecurity can lead to prejudice: When people feel that their livelihoods or their way of life is being threatened, they look for an explanation and, often, for someone to blame. Likewise, emotional insecurity can cause prejudice, as well. Some of the stereotypes we spoke of earlier—that fat people are pathetic; unattractive people are less fun to be with—come out of emotional insecurity.

This sense of insecurity comes from feeling that there is very little that can be counted on or controlled. The teenage years are an especially insecure time for this reason. As teens get closer to adulthood, they develop new bodies, new identities, and new sets of relationships. They have not yet had the years of experience that will reassure them that they can successfully find their own place in the world, their own satisfying romantic and work relationships.

In this context, it may seem like a good idea to "rate" people—both others and oneself—in order to replace the generalized insecurity with a fixed system that seems to offer a "rational" way to determine one's chances of success. Sometimes it feels safer to believe that there are definite standards for social and romantic success—even if those standards are based on stereotypes that aren't really true (attractive people may *not* make the best boyfriends or girlfriends; "unattractive" people may actually be more fun to spend time with). The interesting thing is that people often cling to these stereotypes even at their own expense. Someone who is not super-attractive or especially popular by high school standards may still prefer to believe that the standards are right—just because it feels safer to believe in some kind of rule rather than to judge each person and each situation on its own merits.

The insecurity that leads to rating people on their looks doesn't just come from teenage fears, however. An entire system of advertising plays on people's insecurities about how they look in order to sell more products. Commercials on television and advertisements in magazines continually repeat the message that attractive people are more successful in every way—and that in order to become attractive, you need to buy a certain product. Once again, prejudice turns out not to be a "natural" reaction, but a learned reaction with reasons and explanations we can come to understand.

Explicit Discrimination and Institutionalized Discrimination

In order to understand discrimination, it's important to grasp the difference between discrimination that is consciously practiced and discrimination that seems to happen "by itself," as part of the way that institutions work.

Discrimination resulting from direct expressions of prejudice is often far easier to recognize than discrimination that has become institutionalized. If a particular employer writes a job description that says "No Irish need apply" or "Man wanted for key position," or if the employer directly tells an applicant that a black person will not be considered for a job or that a married person would be preferred, it is fairly easy to recognize that as discrimination. Likewise, if a landlord specifically refuses to rent to a black or Hispanic tenant or to a gay couple his or her prejudice is fairly evident. In the same way, laws that specifically required black people to ride in the backs of buses or that barred Asian people from emigrating into the United States were direct, explicit expressions of prejudice.

Sometimes, however, prejudice and discrimination are far more insidious. They are not necessarily conscious or explicit policies but rather the inevitable results of certain kinds of behavior.

For example, most school systems in the United States are funded by local property taxes. This means that people who live in wealthier neighborhoods are likely to be able to attend better-funded public schools, whereas those who live in poor neighborhoods will be restricted to schools with less money. Since most people in the wealthier neighborhoods are white, and many people in lower-income neighborhoods are from minority groups, minority groups will almost inevitably be restricted to lower-quality public education. No one person has passed a law or made a conscious decision to discriminate against minorities in this way. But the result of the way school systems are funded is that people of one cultural group will get a better education than people of another group. This is known as *institutionalized discrimination*—discrimination that results from the way institutions work. To truly eliminate discrimination, people must address institutionalized racism and prejudice as well as individual attitudes and specific laws.

Here are some more examples of institutionalized discrimination. Can you see how each situation would almost inevitably lead to discrimination?

- Some private social clubs and organizations are the source of many business contacts and networking opportunities, where people can get inside information on jobs and promotions that may be available, cultivate potential customers for their businesses, and make influential friends who can help them in other ways. Most of these clubs are "by invitation only," which means that people invite their friends and relatives to join. In the past, many of these clubs had explicit policies that restricted minorities and Jewish people from joining them; currently, many clubs still have policies barring women. Can you see how even without the clubs' consciously trying to exclude a certain group from business opportunities, discrimination might occur?

- Banks and insurance companies must make decisions about where to invest their assets, where to make loans, and where to support housing construction. To help them make these decisions, they often make use of a practice known as redlining—circling certain sections of a map in red because they have been identified as "bad investments." Sometimes these decisions are made on the basis of zip codes, so that a homeowner in one zip code might be given consideration for a loan that a homeowner in another zip code would not receive. Can you see how, even if race is never mentioned, such a practice could help perpetuate discrimination?

- In order to be successful in the business or sales world, a variety of qualities are needed. In order to manage a department or sell a product, a person must often be forceful and aggressive, as well as perceptive about others, persuasive, and sensitive to how others think and feel. In our society, men are usually seen as forceful and aggressive, whereas women are more often perceived as perceptive and sensitive. How might an ad asking for a "forceful, aggressive salesperson" help perpetuate institutionalized discrimination against women, even if a person's sex or gender is never mentioned in the ad?

The following institutions are often accused of contributing to institutionalized discrimination. Can you imagine why people might make these claims? Remember, institutionalized discrimination takes place when an institution works in such a way as to automatically discriminate against certain people, when a particular group is needlessly kept away from opportunities or advantages even if there is no explicit policy mentioning that group.

- Movie and television studios that assume that some stories are "interesting" and "entertaining" while others are not.
- Book and magazine publishers that consider some writers "prestigious" and other writers "marginal."
- Graduate and professional schools that must make judgments about who is "serious about their study" and "capable of completing the course" and who is not.
- Police and fire departments, who often have height and weight requirements not necessarily related to the demands of the job.
- Voter registration forms that require a great deal of reading to be filled out, that are available only in English, or that must be picked up in particular locations during working hours.

As you can see, in each of these situations, some groups may end up as the targets of discrimination, even if their names are never mentioned in the policies that had that result. If movie studio heads and book publishers are more interested in stories about white characters than minority characters or prefer action-adventure themes that feature brave men rather than human-interest dramas focusing on female characters, women and minority artists and audiences are in effect being discriminated against. This result is even more likely if most of the top executives in these companies are white men because they may be less interested in stories about characters very different from themselves. There is no conscious policy of discrimination—but discrimination may be the result, even if unintentional.

Sometimes, institutionalized discrimination may be hidden behind apparently good reasons for a policy. On the surface, it seems reasonable that graduate and professional schools would require a certain level of dedication in students they accept or that police and fire departments would have certain physical requirements for people they hire.

However, sometimes the requirements only *seem* to have a good reason. Traditionally, for example, medical schools have been intensely competitive. Many women and both male and female doctors have pointed out that some women are uncomfortable with this competitive atmosphere, which does not really foster the skills needed for good medical practice. It is reasonable for a medical school to require a certain academic standard and a certain dedication; however, the assumption that this dedication will take the form of one particular personality type may be an example of institutionalized discrimination.

Likewise, while a police officer or fire fighter certainly needs to display a high degree of physical fitness, some police or fire department regulations have been shown to discriminate needlessly against women. Certain height requirements or the requirement of lifting a certain weight have been shown in some cases to be irrelevant to the actual work that the employees of a particular department do. It would seem that these regulations are more useful at keeping women out of certain jobs, rather than really insuring that employees can meet necessary standards.

It is often difficult to recognize institutionalized discrimination precisely because it is masked with apparently good reasons. In some cases, there may even be good reasons for a particular policy, along with its negative side-effects of discrimination. In other cases, there may be no good reason for a policy, whose main effect may be to perpetuate discriminatory practices in disguise.

Either way, however, if we are going to understand prejudice, we can't just look at the prejudice that individuals express or that laws and policies state explicitly. We must look at all situations that create discrimination—that restrict people from advantages, opportunities, or even necessities on the basis of the group to which they belong.

One of the most insidious parts of institutionalized discrimination is the large number of people it affects. If you are attending a well-funded school system, for example, you are in effect benefiting from institutionalized discrimination against those who are attending less well-funded schools. In a sense, you are benefiting from prejudice, even though you yourself have not necessarily chosen to do so. Likewise, if you are living in a neighborhood that is favored by banks and insurance companies, you are receiving advantages that people in other neighborhoods don't enjoy, even though you haven't chosen to receive the advantages and might even choose to give them up—if you had the choice.

The problem with institutionalized discrimination, of course, is that often individuals don't have a choice about it. Unlike other forms of prejudice, which can be affected by individual decisions, institutionalized discrimination can only be affected by changing the way an institution works. (Of course, any individual can decide that he or she wants to work for such change!)

Hate Crimes and Neighborhood Violence

Prejudice can also take the form of organized violence promoted by hate or "unorganized" or random violence. Members of racial and cultural groups often face physical danger entering certain neighborhoods. In the 1980s, the words *Bensonhurst* and *Howard Beach*—names of all-white neighborhoods in New York City—became symbols of racial prejudice when black passers-by were killed there as a result of white violence. In 1991, police violence against African Americans in Los Angeles became a nationwide scandal, as reports revealed that black people in white neighborhoods were routinely harassed by L.A. police.

Gay people face attacks by "gay-bashers" even in predominantly gay neighborhoods, as well as elsewhere. After the 1970s, when gay people began to insist on not hiding their identities, some groups of young men reacted by seeking out apparently gay men in predominantly gay neighborhoods and harassing or even attacking them. In addition, there have been many incidents of men and women being called names, pushed around, and beaten by people who believed them to be gay or lesbian.

Another type of violence that affects an entire group of people is rape and other forms of sexual attacks against women. This type of violence against women restricts women's freedom in its own way. Rape and sexual attacks can take place anywhere and at any hour of the day or night, and the vast majority of rapes are perpetrated by someone the woman knows. However, many people believe that women can avoid rape by staying out of certain neighborhoods or by not going out alone after a certain hour. This leads women into a double bind: their movement are restricted by this protective "curfew," and then if they are attacked anyway, many people will claim that it was their fault for being in that neighborhood or out at that hour in the first place.

Likewise, many people's response to racial violence or gay-bashing is to suggest that the targets of that violence should voluntarily restrict their own movements. "If they hadn't been in that neighborhood, it wouldn't have happened," was some people's response to the incidents in Howard Beach and Bensonhurst. "If they weren't so blatant about being gay, they wouldn't be attacked," is some people's response to the violence gay people face even in their own neighborhoods.

These responses are themselves a form of prejudice, because they accept the premise that certain people— women, some racial groups, gay people—have fewer rights than others—men, white people, straight people. Of course, given the current climate, everyone must protect himself or herself from potential violence in whatever way seems best. But accepting that some people have the right to visit a certain neighborhood while others do not, or that some people have the right to hold hands with a loved one in public while others do not, or that some people have the right to be out after dark while others do not is accepting prejudice and discrimination.

Becoming Aware of Prejudice

Now that we've seen how widespread prejudice is and how deep it goes, what is the solution? If we are all prejudiced in so many different ways, if we all discriminate against others in some way, if prejudice and discrimination are sometimes not even conscious, how can we ever hope to overcome it?

Recognizing that we all have some prejudices and that many of us may benefit from prejudices against others is a useful first step in understanding prejudice. However, it's helpful to remember that once we understand how prejudice and discrimination work, we all have many choices in how to combat them. Developing this understanding—of our own feelings, of the situations that we're in, of the institutions that shape our lives—is a lifelong process. Whether you are benefiting from prejudice, or are the target of it, or both, there is always more to learn about how prejudice works. And the more you learn, the more choices you will have as to what you can do about it.

Chapters 2 through 5 of this book will go into more detail about different types of prejudice—against racial and cultural groups, against women, against homosexuals, and against the aged and the handicapped—as they have appeared in the United States. Chapter 6 will discuss ways of coping with prejudice through education, as well as through legal and political action. The last chapter will provide the names and addresses of institutions that try to combat various forms of prejudice.

Sometimes learning about prejudice and discrimination can feel uncomfortable. It's not pleasant to find out that you have been the target of discrimination that you had previously ignored. Nor is it pleasant to discover that you have been unconsciously benefiting from someone else's difficulties. These discoveries may make you feel angry, sad, frustrated, confused, or resentful.

However, if you can live with these uncomfortable feelings for a short while, they may inspire you to new insights about how you can combat prejudice and discrimination, by yourself or with a group. And if you see understanding and combating prejudice as a lifelong process, you can be more tolerant of yourself and others as the process of overcoming prejudice continues.

2

Racial and Cultural Prejudice

One of the most destructive types of prejudice is based on someone's race or cultural group. As a nation made up of many different races and cultures, the United States has been marked by racial and cultural prejudice from the very beginning of its history.

Similarities and Differences

On the one hand, racial and cultural prejudice has varied from group to group. The prejudice and discrimination that the Native Americans faced at the hands of the first European settlers was not the same as the prejudices that justified the slavery and segregation of African Americans, and both were different from the varieties of prejudice faced by Hispanic Americans, Asian Americans, Jewish Americans, and Arab Americans.

On the other hand, some aspects of prejudice seem to reoccur. For example, both Asian Americans and Jewish Americans have achieved relatively more economic success than other minority and immigrant groups—and both have been stereotyped as "crafty," "scheming," and "dishonest." Other ethnic labels have shifted from one group to another. The word *guinea*, for example, was an early negative term for black Americans, referring to some black people's origins on the Guinea Coast of Africa. Then, in the 1880s, the term began to be used for Italian Americans, as a derogatory way of saying that they were "no better than black people." The negative word *spic* was originally an insulting label for Italian Americans—but later began to be used to refer to Hispanic Americans.

Likewise, stereotypes and clichés have been "passed" from group to group. As we saw in chapter 1, many groups in America have been stereotyped as "lazy," "criminal," and "immoral": Irish, Jews, Italians, Eastern Europeans, as well as African Americas, Hispanic Americans, and Native Americans. The fact that these stereotypes are so similar tells us that prejudice has more to do with the people who are practicing discrimination than with those who are its targets.

Blaming the Victim

One syndrome that almost all targets of prejudice suffer from is known as "blaming the victim." Blaming the victim is a way of making the targets of prejudice seem responsible for their own difficult circumstances.

For example, suppose a group is discriminated against by being kept out of good schools. Naturally, most of the people in that group would be likely to be less well-educated than people in groups that are not discriminated against. Statistics would probably show that people in the less well-educated group were also less likely to get better-paying jobs that required higher levels of education. Observers might then say, "Well, of course 'those people' don't do well—they should better themselves by going to school!" Instead of recognizing that discrimination is keeping the oppressed group out of school, an observer blames people in the group for not being better educated—and for all the other bad consequences that follow from the initial discrimination.

Because prejudice and discrimination usually take several forms at once, blaming the victim can come to seem logical. In many cases, for example, groups face discrimination both in school and in the job market, and in several other arenas as well. Sometimes, even if a person has gotten a good education, he or she may not do well in the job market because of discrimination. Under those circumstances, even if a person is offered an educational opportunity, he or she might not be able to overcome discrimination in employment. Yet someone who blames the victim might simply say, "Look, even when 'those people' get the chance to go to school, they don't know how to take advantage of it." Instead of seeing through the results of many types of discrimination, a person who blames the victim attempts to reinforce his or her own prejudices and stereotypes.

Hate Groups and Organized Violence

Another result of prejudice is hate groups—groups that have specifically been organized to practice prejudice, discrimination, and violence. All of the racial and cultural groups discussed in this chapter have been the target of hate groups at one time or another. So have Irish, Italian, and Eastern European immigrants. Frequently, a hate group organized to oppose one group goes on to oppose several others as well.

The major terrorist group in the United States is the Ku Klux Klan, a group organized to suppress African American political activity in the years after the Civil War ended in 1865. The Klan was formed by white people who were threatened by the new political rights won by African Americans, who were given full citizenship and voting rights (for men) by the passage of the Fourteenth Amendment (1868) and the Fifteenth Amendment (1870), and who for the first time began to elect political candidates and hold other positions of importance in southern communities.

Members of the Klan would dress in white robes and huge hoods so that they could not be recognized in their illegal activities. Frequently, they raped African American women, burned or looted the property of African Americans, and lynched—hanged—African-American men. Their terror was a constant threat in the south for any African American who wished to express his or her citizens' rights.

The Ku Klux Klan was also opposed to Jewish Americans, Native Americans, and other minority groups. It continues to function today and is still so strong in some communities that in the 1980s a group called Klanwatch was formed to monitor and combat its activities.

Another major hate group is the American Nazi party, inspired in the 1930s by the rise of the Nazi party of Germany. This group believes that an international Jewish conspiracy is responsible for all of America's problems and also believes that African Americans are genetically inferior to white people.

Throughout the 1970s and 1980s, other hate groups formed in the midwest and the south. Many of them have been storing firearms and other weapons with the plan of someday staging a military takeover, or, in some cases, defending themselves against those they fear will attack them. Although each group's political philosophy is different, all see Jewish people and African Americans as a threat to "the rest of America," and some have been charged with various violent crimes against those groups.

Myths and Realities

As we examine the prejudice against various racial and cultural groups, the important thing to keep in mind is how deep stereotypes run and how easy it is to believe in them.

Overcoming prejudice requires seeing through the myths and stereotypes to the facts below. Knowing as much as possible about each cultural group—its history and the type of prejudice directed against it—will help us to cut through the stereotypes and arrive at a better understanding of how prejudice and discrimination work.

Native Americans

Unlike other ethnic groups that now live in the United States, Native Americans were neither brought by force nor did they immigrate here. Instead, they were the original residents of this country, and then the targets of U.S. military efforts to take and keep American lands.

There are many myths and stereotypes about Native Americans, like the ones that follow. How many do you recognize?

Some Common Stereotypes of Native Americans

- They have all disappeared.
- They all live on reservations.
- The ones who live in the cities aren't "really Indian" and have given up their traditions and their Indian identity.
- Indian languages are no longer spoken.
- Indian religions are no longer practiced.
- There is just one "Indian" people.
- Indian culture and religion have stayed the same since the first Europeans arrived here four hundred years ago.

In fact, as we shall see, all of these myths are just that— myths. Not a single one is true.

A Long and Difficult History

Modern American history starts when the first European explorers and settlers arrived in North America in the late

15th century. These early residents came to a land populated by some 2 million to 4.5 million native peoples belonging to hundreds of different nations, each with its own language, religion, and traditions. In fact, there was probably greater variety among Native American cultures of that time than there was among the cultures of Renaissance Europe.

The Europeans had prejudices of their own, however, and they did not see a land with its own cultures and traditions. They saw a group of foreigners living in a rich land filled with resources that they wanted to take. These early Europeans lumped all the Native Americans together, misnaming them "Indians" after the explorer Christopher Columbus's early mistaken belief that he had landed in India rather than in North America.

There are many examples of Indian-European cooperation—the famous Thanksgiving story, Pocahontas's help to explorer John Smith, Sacajawea's assistance in guiding explorers Lewis and Clark in the American Northwest. But from the first, Europeans also looked down on the Native Americans. The first recorded ethnic slur in American English was dated 1699; a British man called a Native American a "redskin."

Besides looking down on Native Americans, Europeans usually treated those peoples with shocking brutality. In the American Southwest and the area that is now Mexico, Spanish conquistadors (conquerors) took advantage of their superior weapons to dominate and destroy Native American civilizations. Although aspects of these ancient cultures persist to this day, the Spanish did everything they could to destroy Native American government and religion as they claimed the land for themselves.

In the northern part of the continent, the French and English colonists treated North America not as a continent inhabited by peoples whose government and customs they must respect, but as a "virgin land," ripe for the taking. Wherever they could, they took Native American lands for themselves.

Throughout the 18th and 19th centuries, the European-American settlers fought with the Native American nations, taking their land and driving them further west. When the railroads wanted to move west in the mid-1800s, they hired men to kill as many buffalo as possible, knowing that the Lakota (Sioux) and other Indians of the Great Plains (the area that stretches through the center of the country, including what are now North and South Dakota, Nebraska, Kansas, Oklahoma, and parts of surrounding states) depended upon the buffalo for their livelihoods. By destroying the buffalo, the railroads were able to drive back the Native Americans.

Although Native Americans were killed outright and starved to death by the loss of their lands or their food supply—such as the buffalo herds—even greater numbers were killed by disease brought by the Europeans. The Native American populations had no resistance to diseases such as small pox, measles, and tuberculosis. Sometimes Europeans deliberately took advantage of this low resistance; for example, by giving Native Americans blankets infected with smallpox. Also, Indian health was severely affected by the brutal conditions of reservation life.

European-American settlers brought destruction to the Native Americans wherever they went. In 1850, there were some 100,000 Native Americans living in California. After the gold rush, however, when thousands of white settlers rushed west to look for gold, the California Native American population had sharply declined—to only 35,000 in 1860.

In 1868, the Civil War had just recently ended. The United States was tired of war and uncertain about continuing a war with Indian nations after the long battle between the North and the South. The U.S. government signed the famous Treaty of 1868 with the Lakota people, granting them the lands that make up North and South Dakota today, as well as parts of neighboring states. This treaty was made between two equal governments—the United States and the Lakota.

Although Native Americans had been driven out of the East and the West of the United States, for a while it looked as though some Indian nations might find peace in the Midwest. Then gold was discovered in the Black Hills of South Dakota—right on sacred Indian land. The United States government wanted to take away the lands that it once agreed to let the Lakota keep. U.S. Army troops broke the peace treaty they had made and went to South Dakota. Although the Indians won the 1876 Battle of Little Big Horn against General George S. Custer, they eventually lost the war. Lakota people of today are still seeking enforcement of the 1868 treaty, through the United Nations.

The U.S. takeover of Indian lands continued. In 1870, the reservation system was set up—a plan whereby Native Americans were granted jurisdiction over territory that nevertheless came under U.S. rule. Instead of being treated as separate nations with whom the United States made treaties, Indians were now treated as American citizens who had the right to live on reservations, which were no more than barren stretches of land that no one else wanted.

Native Americans fought to keep their cultures alive. As you might imagine, over the years, these cultures underwent many changes. For one thing, because of the migrations caused by U.S. expansion, various Indian peoples came together in new ways. There had been confederations and treaties among Indian nations before this, but now that they all faced a common enemy—the United States—they began to work together in new religious and political movements. The Ghost Dance movement of the 1890s, for example, was a political effort undertaken by Indians of several different tribes to preserve Indian religious and spiritual traditions in the face of U.S. efforts to wipe them out.

Native American population in the United States reached its lowest by the end of the 19th century, when various estimates put it at around 250,000. By the mid-1970s, however, it had increased to some 600,000 tribal members recognized by the federal government, plus another 300,000 who consider themselves Native Americans even if not so recognized. According to studies by John H. Price and

Edward A. Spicer, there was a 100% population increase of Native Americans between 1950 and 1970.

Native American Rights and Activism

The 1970s saw a tremendous upsurge in Native American political activism. As with the other minority groups, Indians were inspired by the civil rights movement of the 1950s and 1960s. They began a variety of political and cultural movements, the most famous of which was AIM—the American Indian Movement. These groups faced stiff opposition from the U.S. government in the 1970s, opposition that sometimes amounted to outright war as tanks and helicopters landed on Indian territory in South Dakota or as federal troops and FBI agents were sent to restrain Indian activities.

Native American political movements of today have two focuses. One is to combat the tremendous poverty and economic hardship that have resulted both from direct prejudice and institutionalized discrimination against Native Americans. According to a 1981 study by Alice Kehoe, approximately three-quarters of all Native Americans in the United States are living below the poverty level. Half of the Native Americans counted in the U.S. labor force are unemployed—and many more Indians are never counted in the labor force because they have never worked or have long since stopped trying to get jobs that aren't there. That means that Native Americans have an unemployment rate approximately 12 times that of white, non-Hispanic Americans. The Indian infant mortality rate—the rate at which babies under one year old die—is from 50% to 100% higher than that of white, non-Hispanic Americans. Furthermore, Native American life expectancy—the average length of a person's life—is lower than the national average for all Americans.

Native American political groups have demanded government services, improved education, and economic programs to bring jobs onto reservations. However, they have also served an important cultural purpose. This is the second focus of today's Native American movements. Not just concerned with fighting poverty, these groups are also interested in preserving Native American traditions and religion.

Of course, as we have seen by now, there is no single "Indian" tradition, just as there is no single "European" tradition. Instead, just as we might speak of French, British, Italian, and German customs, we must speak of Lakota, Navajo, Iroquois, or Seminole ways. Yet at the same time, Native Americans in the United States do share some traditions—traditions that have been forged by facing a common enemy. Necessity has made them learn to work together as well as to work to preserve their individual language and religious traditions.

As with other groups, prejudice against the Native Americans often took the form of attacking their cultural and religious traditions. For many years, from the 1920s through the 1970s, a boarding school system often took Indian young people off the reservation and into white-run schools. There they were taught to follow European religions and were forbidden to speak their own languages. This policy gave the message to both Indians and whites that the cultures of the Native American peoples were "inferior" to that of white European Americans. Thus education, religion, and language were the tools of prejudice and discrimination used against the Indian peoples.

Prejudice and discrimination against Indians in America takes many forms today. There is the institutional discrimination of poverty, unemployment, and a low level of government services. There is the specific policy of the reservation system, which has given Native Americans only those poor lands that no one else wanted (although since reservations were established, many have turned out to contain precious minerals, such as uranium, whose ownership is now a new source of controversy).

Yet today, Indian languages are still spoken in the United States, and Indian religious ceremonies are still observed.

Many reservations now seek to maintain their own schools, where they can teach the young about their own history and traditions.

Furthermore, the many Indians who live in the cities as part of a stable working population have also preserved their Indian identities. Many belong to Native American churches, athletic leagues, or other cultural groups. Many have strong and close ties with friends and relatives on the reservation or in rural areas. Contrary to the popular myth that the "real" Indians live on reservations and the Indians in the cities have all become "just like white people," both rural and urban Native Americans have preserved a sense of their heritage, a tradition that, like those of their European neighbors, has changed and grown with the times.

African Americans

In some ways, the very foundation of prejudice and discrimination in the United States was laid with the relationship between European Americans and African Americans. Unlike any other cultural group, African Americans were brought to this country as slaves, and their labor was central to the U.S. economy, first in building the agricultural production of the South, then as the foundation for industrial expansion in the North. Prejudice against African Americans served in some sense as a model for other types of prejudice and discrimination, and African-American movements for equality served as the inspiration for similar movements among other oppressed groups.

To understand the prejudice that African Americans faced, we must first understand what slavery meant. Slavery in North America began in 1607, when the first Africans were brought to this continent, and it continued until the Emancipation Proclamation freed Southern slaves in 1863 and the 13th Amendment to the Constitution formally ended slavery in 1865.

In the United States, slaves were considered less than human, capable of performing certain kinds of work but not capable of or entitled to vote, hold political office, enjoy full legal rights, become educated, or choose where to live. People who were held as slaves were legally defined as property. They did not have the freedom to choose a husband or wife, to raise their own children, or to preserve their families in any way; instead, their owners could decide to marry them to the people of the owners' choice and were always free to sell them, their children, or their spouses to other owners.

The rationale for this treatment of human beings was that certain people were not in fact fully human. Because African Americans had dark skins, skin color was used as the explanation for this subhuman status. As we have seen, earlier societies such as the Romans had had slavery, but they had no such rationales; they simply treated prisoners of war and citizens of conquered nations as slaves. In other words, in that society, you were a slave if you were unlucky enough to lose a battle, not because of any inherent inferiority. In American society, however, slavery was justified as the "natural" lot in life for certain types of people. In fact, many religious and political leaders claimed that enslaving Africans was actually doing them a kindness, by enabling them to leave their own "heathen" religions to become Christian and to leave their own "savage" African nations for the more "civilized" region of North America.

In order to enforce their control over the slaves, slaveowners forbade the practice of African religions and forced conversion to Christianity. Because the slaves came from many different parts of Africa, where different languages were spoken, often their only common language was English. Thus slaves were cut off from their religion, their language, and their culture, and submerged in a culture based on the idea that they were "naturally" inferior to white people.

Nevertheless, African Americans kept elements of their cultures alive, as well as resisting slavery whenever possible.

They organized revolts on slave ships, on the plantations where they worked, and in the regions where they were held. They organized escapes to freedom in the northern United States and in Canada. And free African Americans in the North helped to build the movement known as abolitionism—the movement to abolish, or get rid of, slavery.

After slavery was ended, many African Americans believed that they would finally be given the opportunity to achieve full equality with the white people who had enslaved them for so long. And, for a time, great strides were made. With federal troops stationed in the South to guarantee blacks' political rights, and with federal funds available for education and other services, black Americans made great gains in political representation, entry into the professions, and economic improvement. This period, known as Reconstruction, began when the Civil War ended in 1865.

Then, in 1877, white Southerners succeeded in getting federal troops withdrawn from the South, and Reconstruction was over. As we have seen, terrorist groups such as the Ku Klux Klan mobilized to keep black people from making use of their new legal and political rights. The system known as "Jim Crow" was instituted—an elaborate system of segregation that restricted African Americans in all walks of life throughout the south. Jim Crow laws meant that black people could not ride in the same train cars as white people—nor could they attend the same schools, drink from the same water fountains, use the same public restrooms, or in any way expect the same freedom as white people.

Jim Crow laws had several results. First, they enforced the economic inequality that slavery had begun. At this time, most black people in the South lived in rural areas, working as sharecroppers or tenant farmers. That means that they paid rent to large landowners—either in cash, or in a share of the crop they grew—but owned no land of their own, and so could never advance economically. Black people were restricted from entering many other occupations, and when they were allowed to do other jobs, they were usually paid less than white people for them.

Furthermore, Jim Crow laws reinforced the idea that black people were profoundly inferior to whites. By segregating African Americans, restricting them to inferior facilities, every white person—and every African American—was given the message that poor facilities were all that black people deserved.

Where Jim Crow laws left off, groups like the Ku Klux Klan began. They instituted a system of terror—lynchings, beatings, and other harassment—often in cooperation with police and local officials, to insure that black Americans were not able to exercise political rights or to act as though they were the social equals of white people.

Although conditions were far better in the North, black Americans still faced massive discrimination in employment and education, as well as segregation in many areas of life. Prejudice and discrimination shaped virtually every facet of life for African Americans, whether in the North or in the South.

As industry expanded in the North, African Americans began to leave the South for northern cities, looking for improved opportunities—and the possibility of more social equality. They continued to face prejudice and discrimination of every kind, particularly in the economic arena. In almost every case, black Americans were either restricted from entering certain jobs or were paid less than white people for doing the same job.

Despite the massive prejudice facing them, African Americans managed to achieve an astonishing record of accomplishment. Some entered professional and graduate schools, becoming the few black doctors, lawyers, professors, and scientists of the time. Others became active in political organizing, founding newspapers, starting groups to press for political change, running for political office. Since the entertainment and the sports worlds were rigidly segregated at this time, black Americans responded by organizing their own theatrical productions and their own baseball leagues.

The Civil Rights Movement and Its Aftermath

African Americans have been fighting for freedom and equality since they were first brought to America, but in the late 1950s they achieved a new level of activity—the civil rights movement. This mass movement involved hundreds of thousands of Americans taking new kinds of actions to guarantee full political equality to black people in America. Along with marches, sit-ins, boycotts, and other direct action, civil rights groups registered voters, lobbied elected officials, pursued court actions, and worked for legislation on the federal level to insure that prejudice and discrimination would be ended.

The civil rights movement brought about profound changes in the condition of black Americans. In some ways, these changes can be seen through legislation and court actions. Now public education had to be integrated, black people had to be treated the same as whites at public places like stores and lunch counters, and racial discrimination in employment was outlawed. New laws guaranteed voting rights and new political freedoms, which meant that for the first time since Reconstruction, black candidates were elected to political office and even white candidates had to take black voters into account.

Another result of the civil rights movement was the increase in federal programs to combat poverty, which affected black Americans to a disproportionate extent. However, many of the gains that were won during the 1960s were reversed in the 1970s and 1980s.

Although vast gains have been made, African Americans still face discrimination and prejudice. In 1980, 11.4% of white Americans under 17 were living in poverty—as opposed to 41.6% of black Americans under 17. According to all other indicators, black Americans were earning less than white Americans.

To some extent, this income gap can be explained by differences in education between black and white Americans, a gap that is itself the result of prejudice and discrimination. To some extent, this gap reveals the large number of black families headed by single women—again, a condition that is at least partly the result of the prejudice that makes it difficult for black men to find work, and that puts many young black men at risk of homicide and other types of violent death. This gap can also be explained by the fact that unemployment rates are far higher for black Americans than for whites.

We can see that many of the factors that explain the income gap between black and white Americans are the result of prejudice and discrimination. But to some extent, this income gap must also be considered simply "the cost of being black" because even when such factors do not apply—when you compare only people who have similar levels of education and work experience—white people come out far ahead. In 1959, black men earned only 81% of what white men earned, while black women earned only 53%. In 1979, these figures had not improved much: black men earned 88% of what white men of comparable education were earning, and black women earned only 63%. Thus, even if black people achieve full equality in education, and even if black families were all headed by two adults who could both be earning money, there would still be an income gap between black and white Americans— the "cost of being black."

Evaluating the extent to which African Americans have made progress in overcoming discrimination is an extremely complicated question. Clearly, the fact that Jim Crow laws have been abolished and that it is no longer acceptable to say publicly that black people are inferior human beings represents an enormous advance. On the other hand, despite many gains, prejudice and discrimination continue to mark the lives of African Americans in profound ways.

Hispanic Americans

Hispanic peoples have always played an important part in the history of the United States. As early as the 1500s, Spanish explorers and the colonists settled on the Caribbean islands that are today known as Cuba, the Dominican Republic and Puerto Rico. In the 1700s and 1800s, settlers from Spain came to live in the territory that today is Mexico and the southwestern United States, as well as in South and Central American countries. In 1898, the United States won the Spanish-American War and took the island of Puerto Rico to be its colony, which eventually led to widespread Puerto Rican immigration to the United States in the next century. After the Cuban Revolution of 1959, Cuban emigrés fleeing Fidel Castro's new Communist government were welcomed into the United States. In more recent years, refugees fleeing both poverty and political oppression have come to the United States from Nicaragua, El Salvador, Guatemala, the Dominican Republic, and other Spanish-speaking countries of Central and South America.

When we look at the position of Hispanic Americans and the prejudice they face, we must remember a major difference between Hispanic immigrants and those from Europe. Many Hispanic immigrants came to the United States illegally, at a time when laws severely restricted immigration. Therefore, unlike most of the Europeans, these immigrants were severely limited in the types of jobs they could get and the business opportunities that were open to them, since they had to hide their identities from the authorities in order to avoid being deported (sent back to their own countries).

We also have to keep in mind that there are many different types of Hispanic Americans, from many different cultures, countries, and economic situations. In fact, one of the worst effects of prejudice is the way that it wipes out individual and cultural differences. Somehow, a Puerto Rican garment worker in New York, a Chicano (Mexican American) farm worker in California, and a Cuban-American business owner in Miami are all seen as somehow the same—Hispanic Americans—simply because each comes from a Spanish-speaking culture. To understand the real situation of Hispanic Americans, we have to overcome the prejudice that would lump them all together into a single group.

Many Cultures, Many Experiences

The first Hispanic peoples in the United States came from Mexico. For many years during the 1800s, the United States and Mexico argued and fought over the territory of the southwestern United States. When the current territorial boundaries were finally fixed, United States land included many formerly Mexican citizens.

In addition, Mexicans driven by poverty and the promise of employment migrated from Mexico to California and the Southwest, where they worked for extremely low wages as farm laborers. Because they were so poor, they could be made to work for lower wages than native-born white workers and were used by employers to drive wages down for everyone. Rather than blaming the employers for this policy, white workers often blamed the Mexican immigrants, creating prejudice against Mexicans and Mexican Americans. Ironically, the fact that employers had discriminated against the Mexican migrants in the first place—by paying them lower wages—led to increased prejudice against them as well. Furthermore, small farmers also resented the Mexican immigrants, since they were employed by big farmers who were squeezing the small farmers out of business. Once again, prejudice was used to turn different groups against each other.

Because Mexico and the United States share a border, Mexican immigrants often went back and forth across it, coming to the United States to work, then returning to Mexico to reunite with their families. Frequently, too, Mexican workers were deported, or sent away, especially during the times of year when there was no farm work for them to do.

These conditions made it very difficult for Mexican Americans, or Chicanos, to improve their situation. Both because of direct prejudice and because of the institutional discrimination that had produced their lack of education, they could only get one type of work: seasonal farm work that involved traveling from one region to another, following the work that came each season with the harvest. This migrant lifestyle limited the education that was available for Chicano children continuing the cycle. It also condemned whole families to extreme dependence on the people who hired them and provided them with room and board while they worked, often at exorbitant prices.

Eventually, in the 1950s and 1960s, more Chicanos found jobs in the cities, which offered more access to education and other services. Nevertheless, they continued to suffer from both economic discrimination and the widespread prejudice against Mexican Americans that had developed over the years. Ironically, the stereotypes of Mexican Americans were exactly the same as the myths that had grown up about Irish, Italians, and other immigrant groups of the previous century: lazy, stupid, thinking only of today and never of tomorrow, prone to crafty or criminal behavior rather than to honest work.

European immigrants were able to overcome these stereotypes through the economic success that they achieved. However, Mexican Americans never had the same opportunities as these other immigrants. Instead of working in the cities, they had been restricted to jobs in rural areas, which offered far fewer chances to rise on the social or economic ladder. They had also faced deportation—being sent back to Mexico—during periods of unemployment, which made it even more difficult to establish a stable community that could support small businesses and educational advancement. Given these key differences, it's important not to judge one group by the experience of another.

Another major Hispanic group in the United States are Puerto Ricans, who identify themselves both as U.S. citizens and as people of another land. Many Puerto Ricans would like to see an independent Puerto Rico. Others believe that since the island has been made so dependent on the United States, its ties to the U.S. must continue. Certainly U.S. policy toward Puerto Rico has been a key factor in determining Puerto Rican emigration to the United States. Since the end of World War II in 1945, a full one-third of Puerto Rico's population has left the island to come to the United States, settling mainly in the cities of the Northeast.

Puerto Rican immigrants have also had a different experience than the Europeans who came to this country a hundred years ago. European immigrants came here at a time when industry was expanding rapidly. The opportunities that they found for upward mobility and economic improvement were based on this industrial growth.

Puerto Ricans, on the other hand, have come to the United States during a period of industrial fluctuation and decline. Both Puerto Ricans and the earlier immigrants from Europe got unskilled or semi-skilled jobs in the garment industry, but this industry was prospering from the 1890s to the 1920s, when Europeans arrived—and declining sharply in the 1950s and 1960s, when Puerto Ricans arrived. Furthermore, from the 1950s through the 1980s, U.S. industry tended to move out of the cities and into the suburbs, out of the Northeast and into the Sunbelt, out of the United States and into Mexico, Taiwan, Korea, and other places where wages are low. All of these developments have hurt Puerto Rican immigrants—and have made their experience quite different from that of their earlier European counterparts.

These historical explanations are important to understanding the reality of Hispanic Americans' experience—and to overcoming the prejudice that compares them falsely to other people. Once again, we have an example of "blaming the victim," where a group is prevented from doing well by circumstances and discrimination and then blamed for its own difficulties. Accusing Hispanic Americans of being "lazy" rather than understanding the conditions that prevented them from getting work is a powerful form of prejudice.

The one group of Hispanic Americans that has achieved relative success is Cuban Americans. Their success is based on three factors:

1. They received huge amounts of aid from the federal government, which was eager to welcome refugees from a country whose government it didn't like.

2. Cuban emigrés were leaving their country for political reasons, rather than economic ones. They tended to have far more money saved and to be far better educated than other immigrants.

3. Because of the first two advantages, the Cubans who came to Miami were able to create a whole alternative business community, in which the poor Cuban refugees who followed worked for extremely low wages in the businesses owned by those who were better off. This cheap Cuban labor provided the opportunity for some Cuban business owners to do extremely well. So although Cubans who came to the United States more recently did not usually benefit from the first two advantages, they were able to come to a well-established Cuban community that could provide them with some support.

The Hispanic Americans who come from elsewhere in Central America have none of these advantages. They tend to be poor people who had little education in their own countries. Like Chicanos in the Southwest and Puerto Ricans in the Northeast, they experience prejudice and discrimination in hiring, education, and in the political system. More prejudice and stereotyping—seeing people as "lazy" or "criminal"—leads to blaming people for difficulties they did not create, rather than understanding the true effects of discrimination.

Civil Rights and Political Action

The economic and political problems of Hispanic Americans led to a variety of political movements during the 1970s and

1980s. To some extent, these movements were inspired by the civil rights movement begun by African Americans, which demonstrated the power of collective action to make a difference.

One major movement was the United Farm Workers (UFW), a union of migrant Chicano workers of California led by Cesar Chavez. Farm workers organized for better conditions, higher wages, and the chance to send their children to school. This organization also led to increased political activism among Chicanos in California and in the Southwest.

Another effort took the form of widespread voter registration throughout the Southwest, in an effort to elect Chicano candidates and candidates who would help protect Chicano interests. Political action also increased among Puerto Ricans and other Hispanic Americans in the cities of the Northeast, particularly New York City, home to most Puerto Ricans living in the mainland United States.

Hispanic Americans still face poverty, discrimination, and prejudice. All statistics show that their health problems are greater than those of non-Hispanic white Americans, and their unemployment rates are far higher. Hispanic Americans complete fewer years of school than non-Hispanic white Americans, and, like other minority groups, even when they are well educated, they earn less than non-Hispanic white Americans with similar education. Ironically, the success of one Hispanic-American group—Cuban Americans—has been used to support prejudice, as "proof" that "anyone can make it." As we have seen, however, each Hispanic-American group must be looked at separately, in order to avoid prejudice and stereotyping.

Asian Americans

Asian Americans are in an unusual position relative to other racial and cultural targets of prejudice. On the one hand, they share many of the problems of other non-European immigrants and have done so throughout their history in the United States—discrimination in employment, poverty, cultural stereotyping, etc. On the other hand, some Asian-American groups, particularly the Chinese and Japanese, have done far better economically than other minorities, although they have not quite yet done as well as native-born white Americans. Ironically, the very economic success of Asian Americans has led to different types of prejudice and stereotyping and new types of discrimination.

Immigration, Railroads, and Small Businesses

To understand the nature of prejudice against Asian Americans, we must begin with their history. Asian immigrants have traditionally been a source of cheap labor for the industry and agriculture of the West Coast. Although some Chinese immigrants were drawn to California during the gold rush years of the 1850s, more came later to work as cheap labor on railroads, in mines, in manufacturing industries, and for large landowners who were clearing land and developing the irrigation system that would make California one of the richest agricultural areas in the world.

The first Chinese who came to the United States didn't intend to stay here. They were primarily male peasants who came alone, without their families, and lived as cheaply as possible in this country while sending money back to China. Their intention was always to retire to the village where they had been born, and many of them did leave the United States and return to China. In any case, early immigration laws restricted Asian women from entering the United States, precisely so that Chinese workers could not raise families here.

Because the Chinese were willing to take lower wages than American-born workers, American workers soon developed a strong prejudice against them. The prejudice took the form of legal discrimination: the 1882 Chinese Exclusion Act, which specifically limited immigration from China.

The next wave of immigrants from Asia were therefore the Japanese, who also came to the West Coast as well as to Hawaii. They, too, were primarily male peasants planning to return to Japan, but they had weaker ties to their native villages than the Chinese had. They soon sent for their wives and began establishing families in the United States. They also began what was to become a tradition among Asian immigrants: Some Japanese became self-employed, as truck farmers and in other small businesses, using the unpaid labor of family members to get themselves started.

Once again, native-born Americans saw these immigrants as competition and developed prejudice against them. The "Gentlemen's Agreement" with Japan in 1909 and the Immigration Act of 1924 drastically limited Japanese immigration to the United States.

It is important to note that native-born Americans feared competition from all foreign immigration, because, in general, newly arrived immigrants were always willing to work for lower wages and were used by employers to drive wages down. During the 1920s, a variety of immigration restrictions were passed. However, the restrictions on Asian immigration were especially severe, based on the prejudicial thinking of the time that saw Asians as an inferior and dangerous race. It was around this time that the myths of the "crafty Oriental" and the dangerous "Dragon Lady" took hold as popular stereotypes. Popular literature featured characters like Fu Manchu, the evil but brilliant Oriental scientist. Interestingly, the Asian stereotype always combined both the image of an inferior race— native-born Americans could always outwit them in the end—and a diabolically clever people.

After immigration was cut off from Japan, employers encouraged cheap labor to come from Mexico and from the Philippines. Once again, there was a wave of immigration followed by various laws to limit Asian immigration.

Meanwhile, the Chinese and Japanese immigrants had been in the United States for a few generations. Using both unpaid family labor and cheap, often illegal immigrants from their native countries, some Chinese and Japanese Americans managed to build up small businesses and achieve a certain amount of prosperity. However, their good fortune was built largely outside of the main labor market. Asian immigrants worked at low wages and unskilled jobs either for white Americans or for Asian Americans. Both because of direct prejudice against Asians and because of the institutional discrimination of how the economy worked, they were rarely if ever able to get skilled or managerial jobs in the society as a whole. Their only chance for upward mobility was to start their own businesses using cheap immigrant labor.

During World War II, Japanese Americans faced another type of discrimination. Because America was at war with Japan, many people feared the Japanese living in this country. Once again, this fear was based more on prejudice than on anything else, since America was also at war with Germany and Italy, yet there was much less fear of German Americans or Italian Americans. People's myths and stereotypes about "evil Asians" led to laws that allowed Japanese Americans' property to be confiscated and Japanese Americans to be imprisoned in detention camps. Ironically, the sons of these Americans were often fighting in the U.S. Armed Forces for the country that was imprisoning their families, simply on the basis of their nationality.

After World War II, the earlier acts against Asian immigration were still in place, perpetuating that form of discrimination. Finally, a new immigration act in 1965 eliminated the racially motivated barriers to Asian immigration. New immigrants entering the United States from Korea, Hong Kong, Taiwan, and India tended to be very different from the peasants and unemployed workers who had made up most European and Asian immigration in the past. These new immigrants were from urban families that included a high proportion of college-educated professionals and white-collar workers. The new Asian immigrants from these countries came to the United States with far more advantages than any other immigrant group had ever brought. Of course, other Asian immigrants—such as Vietnamese, Cambodia's Hmong, Thais, and others from Southeast Asia—were more likely to be poor and uneducated.

As you can see, Asian immigration to the United States included many factors that reflected prejudice and discrimination. Ironically, it also included many factors that allowed some Asians to achieve a measure of economic success. Precisely because Asians were discriminated against in the rest of the labor market, they were available to work as cheap labor for those Asian employers who managed to go into business for themselves. Meanwhile, Asians continued to suffer from social discrimination—negative stereotypes in books and movies, unequal treatment by schools and storeowners, exclusion from political activity, etc.

Economic Success and the "Cost of Being Asian"

Today, the three major Asian immigrant groups in the United States are the Chinese, Japanese, and Filipinos (people from the Philippines). There are also Asian immigrants from Korea, Hong Kong, India, and Southeast Asia. Each of these groups has quite a different economic position.

The Chinese Americans and Japanese Americans have been the most successful economically. Part of their success probably comes from their high concentration in California, an unusually prosperous state. Another reason for their success has to do with their high levels of education. In addition, the growing number of Japanese-owned businesses located in California means that Japanese Americans have increased access to high paid employment as managers and technical personnel.

A 1979 study by Victor Nee and Jimmy Sanders of Asian Americans in California showed that Chinese Americans and Japanese Americans had achieved equal or even slightly greater proportions of administrative, technical, or professional jobs as native-born white Americans. They also found that Chinese Americans and Japanese Americans had earnings that were comparable to those of native-born white Americans.

However, even among these successful groups, Nee and Sanders found that white Americans still had an advantage. When they compared college-educated whites with college-educated Asian Americans, they found that whites averaged over $4,000 a year more than their Japanese-American counterparts, over $6,000 a year more than college-educated Chinese Americans, and over $9,000 a year more than college-educated Filipinos. These figures might be called "the cost of being Asian." In other words, despite the enormous economic progress of this most successful "minority" group, racial prejudice still seems to play a role.

Furthermore, other Asian groups have not been as successful as Chinese and Japanese Americans. Filipino Americans, in particular, seemed to be confined far more to working-class jobs and lower incomes. Although as a group Filipino Americans were less well-educated than Chinese and Japanese Americas, even those Filipino Americans who did have college degrees seemed to benefit less from them than other Asian Americans—and certainly far less than did white Americans.

Ironically, the very economic success of some Asian Americans has created resentment against all Asian Americans, who are often stereotyped as "too powerful" or labeled with updated versions of the myth of the clever but evil Asian. This has sometimes led to outright violence against Asian Americans. As the country of Japan has continued to improve its economic status in the world at large, many white Americans associate economic success with all Asian Americans, even though many Asian Americans are not Japanese and those who are do not necessarily benefit from Japan's success.

Overcoming prejudice against Asian Americans requires a good deal of careful thinking because reality is so much more complicated than the myths and stereotypes that abound. Even if some Asian Americans have been highly successful, they still face discrimination, both "the cost of being Asian" and the violence that comes from fear and resentment. Other Asian Americans, such as those from India and Korea, have managed to build up some small successes with small businesses, using unpaid family labor, cheap immigrant labor, and savings from their households in their native countries—but even they have not achieved the high incomes and economic security of well-paid, college-educated professionals. Still other Asian Americans, particularly those with peasant backgrounds and little education, have not been able to overcome prejudice and poverty.

Jewish Americans

Like Asian Americans, Jewish Americans are often cited as being "the minority that made it." Various studies have shown that Jewish median income is higher than the national average, certainly higher than that of other ethnic minorities or immigrant groups. Many Jewish Americans have achieved national prominence as figures in the arts and entertainment world, as Nobel Prize–winning scientists, or as presidential advisors. In popular myths and stereotypes, Jewish Americans' commitment to education and willingness to work hard created their amazing "success story."

In fact, the truth is actually much more complicated. First of all, despite their apparent success, Jewish Americans are still the targets of prejudice and discrimination. Second, the reasons for Jewish-American success have much less to do with cultural factors such as "love of education" and "hard work" than with economic factors, such as the skills that Jews brought with them when they emigrated.

Immigration, Anti-Semitism, and Success

Jewish Americans faced anti-Semitism (prejudice against Jews) from the moment they first set foot in America, starting with New York Governor Peter Stuyvesant's unwillingness to let Jews enter the Port of New York in 1654. Various political movements in the 1800s, such as the Know Nothing party of the 1850s and the Populist movement of the 1890s, explicitly blamed Jews for many of the nation's troubles.

The Jews who first came to the United State in large numbers were the German Jews who came in the 1850s. They tended to be well educated and from somewhat middle-class backgrounds. This period was a time when some individuals were able to make huge fortunes in banking, trading, and finance. Just as John D. Rockefeller and Andrew Carnegie rose to become millionaires, so did some German-Jewish Americans, who founded some of the great financial houses of Wall Street.

The next wave of Jewish immigration came in the 1890s, when hundreds of thousands of workers and peasants from southern and eastern Europe entered the United States to work for low wages in U.S. factories and workshops. This was a time of intense prejudice against newcomers, and newly arrived Jewish Americans faced their share of stereotyping and discrimination. It is difficult to measure whether anti-Semitism was stronger, weaker, or about the same as anti-Italian or anti-Polish feeling of the time, but there are certainly striking examples of it. For example, in 1890, New York City Police Commissioner Theodore Bingham complained that half of all criminals in the city were Jews.

Jewish Americans were, like other immigrants, stereotyped as being criminal elements, dangerous, and incapable of fitting into the "civilized" American way of life. Jews were also stereotyped in more specific ways: as frauds and cheats who manipulated the law and engaged in clever schemes to get ahead. In many ways, the stereotypes of clever Jews and clever Asians were strikingly similar.

Despite the stereotypes, however, there was little direct discrimination against Jews. Only 0.3% of the want ads before World War I specified wanting "Christian" employees, and colleges and universities had no formal entrance barriers against Jewish students. During this time, by comparison, Native Americans were being herded onto reservations; Asian Americans were being excluded from immigrating to the United States; African Americans were being restricted by Jim Crow laws of segregation; and immigration laws were restricting immigration of Polish and Italian natives.

Jewish immigrants, meanwhile, were enjoying certain advantages in the American economy. As compared to other immigrants, they were a largely urban group, having more experience with cities and towns than the Italian and Eastern European peasants who came to the United States. Jews' urban experience was partly a result of discrimination in Eastern Europe, where they were often not allowed to own land or were driven off their land by anti-Jewish riots called *pogroms*. Ironically, this very discrimination gave them an opportunity for another type of experience that was to prove valuable in America.

Furthermore, because they were restricted from so many other jobs, it happened that European Jews were skilled in the garment trades. This field, made possible by Isaac Singer's new sewing machines of the 1880s, was rapidly expanding in the 1890s and early 1900s. Thus, Jews who were already skilled in the garment trades had a natural advantage over other immigrants when they came to the United States.

Possibly because of Jewish-American success in this industry, anti-Semitism increased after World War I. By 1920, 10% of all want ads specified wanting Christian employees, and by 1926, the figure was up to 13.3%. Colleges and universities, including the prestigious Columbia and Harvard, began to restrict the number of Jews they would admit as students. Industrialist Henry Ford began printing statements that held an international Jewish conspiracy of financiers and bankers responsible for the difficulties in American industry, while Wisconsin Senator Robert M. La Follette introduced a 1923 petition to Congress holding Jewish bankers responsible for World War I and claiming that the leaders who had negotiated that war's peace treaty were all surrounded by Jewish advisors.

The myths and stereotypes used to justify prejudice against Jews were thus quite contradictory. On the one hand, Jews were said to be petty criminals, scheming and thieving, and lacking the high moral character to become "real" Americans. On the other hand, they were extremely powerful, engaged in an international conspiracy to destroy America.

To a great extent, these myths and stereotypes persist today. Organized anti-Semitic hate groups depend on this stereotype. On the other hand, we also have today the stereotype of the dedicated Jewish immigrant, who by hard work and education managed to succeed where others failed. This myth is often used to criticize other immigrant groups who have not been so successful.

Of course, the Jewish Americans who did achieve economic and social success were hard-working and dedicated. But so were countless other immigrants and African Americans. The differences among the various groups cannot be explained by myths and stereotypes about "hard work" or "education," but rather by the different circumstances that each group happened to face.

Regardless of economic achievement, Jewish Americans faced a wide range of prejudice throughout the 1930s, 1940s, and 1950s. Many graduate and professional schools continued to maintain quotas—limits on the number of Jews they would accept. Many neighborhoods were "restricted"; that is, it was legal to put in the deed to a house or a piece of land the restriction that it could not be sold to a Jew. Likewise, many social clubs and country clubs would not accept

Jewish members. Stereotypes were continually used to justify this prejudice: the claim that Jews were "pushy," "loud," "unpleasant," "dishonest," and somehow "un-American."

These stereotypes were often supported by pointing to the next wave of European Jews that had entered the United States. Ironically, these Jews were fleeing the most intense anti-Semitic prejudice that the world has ever known: the efforts of German dictator Adolf Hitler to literally destroy every Jew in Europe in his infamous concentration camps. Although few Jews were able to escape Hitler's rule in Germany and Eastern Europe, many of those who did sought to come to the United States—but were restricted by quotas on immigration. After the war, many more Jews sought to leave the Europe that had been the site of so much destruction, frequently emigrating either to the United States or to the new nation of Israel.

Anti-Semitic prejudice has decreased enormously in the last two decades, but as we have seen, some hate groups still make use of these stereotypes, and anti-Semitic ideas are still expressed from time to time. Furthermore, incidents of anti-Jewish violence continue, including burning and vandalizing Jewish synagogues and defacing Jewish cemeteries. Both Asian Americans and Jewish Americans have seen that a measure of economic success is not sufficient defense against the violence and abuse that prejudice breeds.

Arab Americans

In recent years, a new type of prejudice has become widespread in the United States: prejudice against Arab Americans. Like Asian Americans and Hispanic Americans, Arab Americans come from many different countries and cultures but tend to be lumped together into a single group by those whose prejudice keeps them from paying attention to these important differences.

Prejudice against Arab Americans has been inspired by two types of political events: Israel's conflict with Arab nations in the Middle East, and the United States' conflicts with the oil-producing nations of the Middle East, as well as with the countries of Iran and Iraq. Ironically, Iran is not even an Arab nation—Iranians are more closely related to Indians and Pakistanis, and their language is closer to the languages of India and Europe than to the Arabic spoken elsewhere in the Middle East. Once again, prejudice leads many people to overlook real differences in favor of a generalized stereotype.

In recent years, Arab Americans have been made the target of people's resentment against the policies of various Middle Eastern nations. Just as Asian Americans have suffered from the perception that Japan's economic growth has hurt the United States, Arab Americans have been blamed for high oil prices or for Iran's taking of American hostages. During the recent U.S. war with Iraq, there were many reported incidents of Arab Americans being beaten or harassed—even those who were not even of Iraqi descent and despite the fact that they were not in any way responsible for the policies of a foreign government.

3

Prejudice Against Women

Understanding prejudice against women raises a number of interesting questions. Because people have so many theories about the differences between men and women, they do not always agree on what constitutes prejudice and what is simply recognizing the real differences between the two sexes.

Following are a number of common situations that women frequently face. The examples themselves are composites—drawn from many different situations that represent common circumstances. Which examples do you think represent discrimination and prejudice?

- Liz works as a secretary for the city parks department. She earns $500 a week. José is a maintenance man for the same office. He earns $750 a week.
- Whenever 18-year-old Tina is out after dark, she makes sure to either get a ride or find a friend to walk with. When she's leaving a friend's house, she calls home to let her parents know she's coming and what time she expects to get home. Sometimes Tina just feels like

getting out by herself and going to a movie or taking a walk, but she has no car and isn't allowed to take the bus downtown by herself after dark. Her 16-year-old brother, on the other hand, comes and goes freely, as long as he's home by their 10 o'clock curfew. When Tina complains to her parents, they say, "Things could happen to you that couldn't happen to him."

- Joanna likes her job as a newspaper reporter, but she's not so crazy about her boss. He's always coming by her desk to tell her how nice she looks, leaning over her shoulder to see what she's working on, and putting his hand on her shoulder just a little too long. She's tried to brush him away or make a joke out of it, but then he gets hurt and upset. Lately he's been hinting that he'd like to ask her out. Joanna isn't interested, but she isn't sure how he'll react if she simply says "no."
- Rita has two kids, age 6 and 5. She and their father got divorced two years ago, and he sends money when he can, but he isn't doing too well either. The children are in school but get home by 3 o'clock. Rita is a trained paralegal and would like to get a job in a law office, but what would she do with her kids? The only work she can get that fits her kids' schedule is waitressing, which doesn't pay very well. If she can't get a job that can support three people, she'll have to go on welfare.
- Margo is a lawyer and has been with her firm for six years. Now she's 32 and she and her husband, who's also a lawyer, want to have a baby. Neither of them wants to put an infant in full-time day care, especially since they would both like Margo to breast-feed the baby for several months. Margo's husband isn't sure his firm will let him work part-time. Even if it does, he's afraid this will take him off the track for further promotions. Margo is afraid that the same will apply to her. She knows that if she takes a year off, she can probably find another job, but she will have lost her six years' seniority with her old firm and may never again be on the same promotion track.

- Ellen and Tom are both entering freshmen at the state university. Their advisors ask them what they plan to major in. Ellen can't make up her mind between social work and English literature. Tom is torn between engineering and accounting.
- Angela has been working for four years at a small firm. She is now paid $30,000 a year. Carl joins the firm and Angela's boss asks her to give him a few pointers. One day, when Angela and Carl are both complaining about making ends meet, Angela finds out that Carl is making $36,000 a year. When she goes to her boss to complain, he says, "But he has a family to support." A few months later, there is an opening for a promotion—and Carl gets it. When Angela complains, she is told, "You'll be leaving soon to get married and have children. We need somebody we can count on."

Understanding Prejudice Against Women

As these examples show, the question of prejudice against women is a complicated one, although some situations may appear more clear-cut than others.

"Equal Pay for Equal Work"

For example, these days, most people would agree that Angela's story is an obvious case of discrimination. She and a man are doing exactly the same work—in fact, she is so experienced that she is helping to train the man. Yet he is earning more money that she is, simply because he's a man. Today, this type of discrimination is illegal, and if Angela can prove that she has gotten less money or less of a chance at a promotion simply because she's a woman, she can bring a lawsuit against the company. Yet for many years, many people believed that it was right for men to earn more money than women for the same work. The slogan "Equal pay for equal work" was considered quite controversial.

Even today, it's quite difficult for a woman to prove that she has been discriminated against in this way. Yet, according to sociologist Robert Cherry, this type of outright discrimination against women probably accounts for at least half of the difference between men's and women's average yearly earnings.

Comparable Worth

Liz's case is more complicated. She is doing a different type of job from José, so at first glance, it might seem appropriate for her to be getting a different salary. Yet a closer look raises different questions. Why is a secretary's work less valuable than a maintenance man's?

In recent years, this issue has become known as *comparable worth*; that is, the question of how you compare the worth of two different types of jobs—one of which is done almost exclusively by men at higher pay, the other of which is done almost exclusively by women at lower pay. One study of the Rockford, Illinois Housing Authority, for example, cited by Gabrielle I. Edwards in *Coping With Discrimination*, found that 85% of the maintenance staff was male. Although both types of work were necessary to the operation of the office as a whole, the type done primarily by men was far better paid than the type done primarily by women.

Many people would argue that the major reason for this difference is prejudice against women—the view that any work a woman does is automatically less valuable than work done by a man. Prejudice against women may also help explain why women choose "female" jobs like secretarial work rather than "male" jobs like maintenance work—and why employers would rather hire women secretaries and male maintenance crews.

Everyone agrees that women in the United States earn far less than men. A 1984 study by Earl Miller published in *Monthly Labor Review* showed that even when he compared only men and women with similar educations and work experience, women still earned less than 70% of what men earned. Some of this gap may be explained by cases like Angela's, where women are doing the same jobs as men and simply getting less money for them. Some of the gap may be explained by cases like Liz's, where women tend to work in lower-paid, traditionally female occupations.

Child-Rearing, Day Care, and Seniority

Some of the gap may also be explained by cases like Rita's and Margo's, where women end up with extra responsibilities for child-rearing that men do not have, responsibilities that affect their seniority, chances for promotion, and all-around earning power.

In Rita's case, prejudice against women may be taking the form of institutional discrimination. Imagine how different Rita's situation would be if she could work at a law office with its own day-care center, or if she had access to a government-subsidized day-care center in her neighborhood. She would have a place to leave her children while she worked, rather than being condemned to going on welfare or finding jobs that allow her to be home at 3 o'clock.

We might also look at the institutional discrimination of companies themselves, most of which do not offer part-time work with benefits or flexible hours to accommodate women with children. Since in our society, the responsibility for raising children usually does rest with the woman, failing to provide support for child-rearing is a form of institutional discrimination against women.

Further, we might ask to what extent prejudice against women is itself behind the fact that women rather than men usually have the responsibility for raising children. Perhaps Rita prefers to have her children with her all the time. Perhaps, though, she might like an arrangement where her children could be with her part of the time and with their father the other part of the time. Maybe prejudice against women has helped plant in Rita's mind the idea that any woman who is not with her children all the time is a "bad mother," or perhaps she is afraid that others may call her a "bad mother." Rita may be freely choosing to take on the sole responsibility for her children—or her choices may be shaped by a climate of prejudice and discrimination.

Likewise, in Margo's case, we can see how the apparently free choices that she and her husband make are shaped by institutional discrimination on many levels. If Margo and her husband "decide" that she should take a year off work, Margo will lose seniority and chances at promotion, another part of the gap between men's and women's incomes. The lack of flexible hours, available day care, or tolerance for Margo's husband taking on less work and more child-care responsibilities all contribute to a form of institutionalized discrimination against women. That is, the way existing institutions are set up, Margo is quite likely to end up earning less money and working in a lower position than her husband—and so is virtually every other married woman who wants to have children. Although no one is saying directly, "Women must earn less than men," every part of the situation is set up in a way that practically guarantees that that's how it will turn out.

Feminists—people concerned with women's rights—have proposed a number of institutional changes to combat this problem. First, they suggest that part-time work with no loss in seniority or benefits be made available to both men and women, so that two-parent families will have the option of two adults working part-time or of one adult working part-time with the ability to get back on a promotion track when the children are older. Second, they suggest that both employers and the government help provide affordable, quality day care. Can you think of other institutional changes that would address this type of discrimination?

Sexual Harassment

Joanna faces a different problem, one known as *sexual harassment*. Sexual harassment takes place whenever an employee is subjected to unwanted sexual advances or sexual attention and does not have the power to demand that the advances stop. Sometimes an employer will literally make sexual favors a requirement for keeping a job or for getting a promotion. Sometimes an employer simply insists on his (or her) right to make sexual remarks or act in a sexual way, even if the employee finds this intrusive or embarrassing.

According to Title VII of the 1964 Civil Rights Act, all employees have the right to be free of sexual harassment, which the act defines as follows:

> Unwelcome sexual advances, requests for sexual favors, and other verbal and physical conduct of a sexual nature . . . when
> - submission to such conduct is made a term or condition of an individual's employment,
> - submission to or rejection of such conduct is used as the basis for promotional decision, or
> - such conduct unreasonably interferes with work performance, or creates an intimidating, hostile, or offensive working environment.

According to Gabrielle I. Edwards in *Coping with Discrimination*, almost 50% of all working women have been subjected to sexual harassment. Some observers believe that whenever men and women work together, it is possible to find at least one example of sexual harassment.

Sexual harassment has many effects on women, some obvious, some less so. In the most obvious cases, an employer's harassment might be the cause of a woman losing a job or a chance at promotion. Harassment might also make a workplace so uncomfortable that a woman employee would feel compelled to leave her job and find another—even though she has done nothing wrong and might prefer to keep her job.

On a more subtle level, sexual harassment gives a profoundly damaging message to women employees. It reinforces the idea that they are being hired not to do a job, as a man is hired, but instead to please a man, to be a kind of "office wife." Sexual harassment gives the message that, instead of having the freedom to come to work, to do a job well, and be recognized for one's work, a woman must always be thinking about pleasing men. Young women, in particular, feel that sexual harassment undermines their sense of themselves as competent workers, reinforcing instead the idea that all they have to offer is a cute smile or an attractive figure.

Because sexual harassment may take subtle forms, as in Joanna's case, many women do not even realize that they are being sexually harassed, or, if they do realize it, have difficulty in convincing others that this is indeed the situation. When Joanna complains to her boss, he denies that he is doing anything—but then acts hurt and angry. Since he has the power to fire or to promote her, his reactions matter much more to Joanna than those of some other man she might decide not to go out with.

Sometimes women who are being sexually harassed ask themselves if they are causing the situation. They may alter their appearance to look less sexual or less attractive, try to avoid the harasser, or make sure never to be alone with him. These efforts all put an added strain on a work situation. This strain is a form of discrimination, since in most cases male employees do not have to deal with it. (Now that there are more female bosses and supervisors, male employees are occasionally subject to sexual harassment; they may also be harassed by gay male employers or supervisors. However, these cases are extremely rare compared to male-female sexual harassment.) Sometimes the strain of sexual harassment produces headaches, stomachaches, back problems, high blood pressure, ulcers, or other stress-related illnesses.

Violence Against Women

When Tina complains that her parents are "discriminating" against her by not letting her go out alone after dark while permitting her younger brother to do so, her parents feel justified in replying, "You are in more danger than your brother." They might point to the statistics cited by Gabrielle I. Edwards in *Coping With Discrimination*: In the United States, one woman is raped every 3 seconds. Of these, one in three is raped by a stranger, whereas two-thirds are raped by people they know. One woman in seven is raped by her husband.

To respond to this horrifying reality, Tina may have to take some steps to protect herself that are not necessary for her brother. She may take the precautions her parents recommend, enroll in a self-defense class, or decide on other ways to guard her safety.

Beyond simply responding to a bad situation, however, Tina, like many other women, may choose to see the problem as another example of prejudice against women. Feminists have argued extensively among themselves over what creates rape and violence against women, and there is deep disagreement over how these problems can be solved. All agree, however, that just as people of color should have the right to go into the same neighborhoods and public places as white people, so women should have the right to be out in public at the same hours of the day or night as men. To the extent that women cannot exercise this right, they are facing a profound form of discrimination.

Some feminists argue that rape and other violence against women is caused by a climate of opinion that insists that women are "good for only one thing"—to serve men's sexual pleasure. Others believe that such violence is encouraged by films, television, and books, which continue to portray rape and other violent crimes, frequently in an exciting or even a glamorous way. In a famous scene from the movie *Gone with the Wind*, for example, a man is shown forcing himself on a woman sexually. At the time, she resists, but afterwards, she is shown with a smile on her face, having thoroughly enjoyed the "romantic" sexual encounter. Feminist media critics say that such scenes give both men and women the message that forced sex is a form of love, whereas it is really a form of violence.

Still others suggest that rape and violence toward women are supported by thinking that "might makes right." When men feel powerless or frustrated, they look for someone weaker than themselves to take their frustrations out on—and since women are seen as weaker than men, and are frequently physically not as strong, they are often the targets. This view is supported to some extent by some statistics, which might seem to suggest that rape and other violent crimes increase when unemployment rates go up. However, this statistical evidence is unclear and no one is quite sure how to interpret it.

Besides the violent crime of rape, women also face the crime of *battering*, being beaten up. This crime usually takes place between a woman and her husband or boyfriend. Frequently, battered women are in a vicious cycle in which they are beaten and then threatened with worse punishment if they report the beatings. Occasionally a man will beat a woman and then express deep remorse, begging for her forgiveness and promising never to do it again.

Women stay with battering men for a variety of reasons. Sometimes they believe the threats and are afraid of being hurt worse if they resist or leave the man. Sometimes they love the man who beats them and want desperately to believe that he can change. Sometimes they have children whom they cannot support alone or are financially dependent upon the man in other ways. Sometimes they are affected by a combination of these circumstances—fear, love, dependence, plus fear of what they would do if they were on their own.

These problems are compounded by the fact that it is very difficult to jail a man who is battering a woman, particularly if she is his wife, since there are rarely adult witnesses to the crime. Furthermore, jail sentences for so-called domestic disputes are usually not very long. A woman might well fear that a man whom she had helped send to jail for beating her would return, more angry than ever. Under such circumstances, a woman might not choose to press charges, especially if she also believes that she loves the man or needs his financial support in raising their children. Once again, we can see the intersection between what appear to be "free" choices and the climate of prejudice and discrimination that shape those choices.

Choosing Careers

Certainly Ellen's wish to major in English or social work and Tom's interest in engineering or accounting would seem to be free choices. Each person "just happens" to be pursuing his or her interests. However,when we realize that Ellen, like most girls, has "just happened" to choose low-paying fields whereas Tom, like most boys, has "just happened" to choose higher-paying ones, we can imagine that institutional discrimination and prejudice may be at work once again.

According to Gabrielle I. Edwards in *Coping With Discrimination*, women are nearly 50% of the U.S. workforce but only 6% of the research or teaching scientists and engineers. According to a 1977 National Center for Educational Statistics report, in 1975, 64.3% of female college graduates in the United States majored in education, social science, literature, fine arts, or health—all fields that lead to far lower-paid jobs than degrees in business, science, or engineering. The same study showed that 30% of the men chose business and engineering majors—whereas only 5% of the women did so.

Even in 1988, women were still underrepresented in the more lucrative fields. In that year, according to the U.S. Department of Education, only 14.9% of the engineering majors at four-year institutions of higher education were women, and only 34.9% of the pre-med students. Although 45.4% of the business students and 42.2% of the pre-law students were women, only 28.8% of the physical science students and only 37.7% of the architecture students were women.

How do women come to make these choices? Dr. Jane Butler of Purdue University conducted a study of high school and college girls in which she found the following factors: Their parents didn't value science education for them; they themselves had negative attitudes towards science; teachers were more interested in male students; and girls had no role models—no successful adult women—in physics, chemistry, and geology.

In a climate where almost no women are seen to be practicing or teaching science, it might require an unusual amount of interest and dedication for a girl to decide to make science her career. If the male teachers and classmates she encounters share the general feeling that she is in a "man's field," she will have to overcome their doubts as well as her own if she is to pursue this difficult but rewarding field. These self-doubts and external obstacles are problems that a man considering a career in science or engineering does not have to face. Thus, they represent another form of institutional discrimination against women, with the result that there are in fact far fewer women in science than men.

The same dynamic field is likely to operate in business, accounting, and every other field generally perceived as a "man's field." Many adult women, reflecting on their career choices, say that it simply never occurred to them to consider science, business, or some other "man's profession." Others say that they were afraid of the pressure, the competition, or the disapproval of family, friends, boyfriend or husband. Certainly these women bear some responsibility for the choices they made—but we need also to look at the climate of prejudice in which they made their decisions.

Women and Biology

When discussing prejudice and discrimination against women, many people will bring up the question of biology. They point out that men and women are biologically different and suggest that there may be good scientific reasons for the differences in their behavior. Biology has been called on

as an explanation for everything from women's responsibility for child-rearing to women preferring literature
over science to men's "drive" to rape or treat women
with violence.

The question of biology is indeed a complicated one. At
this time, scientists generally agree that there are many
biological differences between men and women, extending
to hormonal reactions and metabolism as well as to the
obvious differences of primary and secondary sex organs.
What no one can agree on, however, is the ways in which
biological differences translate into differences in feelings,
desires, or behavior.

One famous study of infant boys and girls, for example,
found that baby girls have a far higher rate of smile reflexes
than baby boys. Some scientists immediately claimed this as
proof that women are biologically programmed to be more
accommodating than men. Other scientists suggested that
perhaps women were biologically programmed to be more
outgoing or more self-confident, meeting the world with a
smile. Still other scientists pointed out that we don't really
know what smile reflexes signify in infants who are too
young to *choose* to smile at anyone, but are merely experi-
encing smile reflexes as some kind of biological reaction.

Supposedly scientific theories about women that were
once commonly accepted are now seen as ridiculous and
farfetched. As recently as 30 years ago, for example, some
doctors believed that it was dangerous for girls to shower or
bathe while they had their periods because the loss of blood
might cause them to faint. In the Victorian era of the 1890s,
upper-class women who were pregnant were "confined"—
kept indoors, in bed, if possible, during their entire pregnancy. (Of course, pregnant working-class women
continued to work and to take care of their children as
usual!) Because Victorians saw women as fragile and pregnancy as woman's highest mission, they developed "scientific" theories to support these prejudices. Nowadays, we
would see their "medical" advice as pure superstition, rec-

ognizing that, in most cases, it's healthier for a pregnant woman to stay active.

Our grasp of biology will doubtless continue to grow over the years. Our interpretations of biological data will also doubtless change to fit our new ideas and outlooks. Meanwhile, it's good to be aware that biology has been used in the past to "prove" many points that we no longer accept as true and to remember that there is still a great deal of disagreement over what biology can tell us about the feelings and behavior of men and women.

Women's Rights— A Long Struggle

What we take for granted about women's rights has changed enormously over the years, particularly in the last 20 years. Which of the items on the following list do you take for granted? Which statements seem strange to you?

- Women should be able to vote.
- Women are qualified to serve in juries.
- Women can hold political office.
- I expect to see a woman announcer on the nightly news and to read stories by women reporters in the daily newspaper.
- I can easily imagine a woman working as a doctor or a lawyer.
- With the right training, a woman can be an astronaut.
- Most women expect to work for most of their adult lives, even if they have children.

Today, these statements about women's rights and abilities seem commonplace. Yet 20 years ago, it was still highly unusual for married women and women with children to hold jobs outside the home. There were few women's faces on television news and few women's bylines in the daily newspaper, and 30 years ago, there were virtually none at all. Twenty years ago, a woman astronaut was inconceivable in the United States (although there had been women cosmonauts in the Soviet Union). Although women might work as doctors or lawyers, they were extremely rare, and successful women professionals were rarely portrayed on television or in the movies.

Going back 70 years, to the 1920s, we find a time when women were not allowed to vote in national elections and so could not run for political office or sit on juries. The movement that fought to win voting rights for women began in 1848—and struggled for almost 80 years before finally achieving success.

The year of 1848 was in fact the beginning of the first American women's movement. Before that year, it was generally accepted that women had no political rights. They were viewed as their fathers' responsibilities before marriage and their husbands' responsibilities after it. A married woman might not control her own property and might find it extremely difficult to initiate a divorce, even if her husband had deserted her, was unfaithful to her, or regularly abused her. In any case, a divorced woman was extremely vulnerable, since there were virtually no jobs or professions open to women, although women might work on family farms or in family businesses owned and run by men. Women might also work as governesses, school teachers, or domestic servants—but only until they got married.

In the early 19th century, more jobs opened up for women as industrial development created factories and mills that needed cheap labor. The "mill girls" of the textile mills in Lowell, Massachusetts, were an early example of women working in jobs outside the home. Although these jobs were often difficult and dangerous, and invariably paid women lower wages than were paid to men, nevertheless they were the beginning of new possibilities for women in the workforce outside the home.

In 1848, Susan B. Anthony, Lucretia Mott, Elizabeth Cady Stanton, Lucy Stone, and other pioneering feminists called the first U.S. conference on women's rights. These women had been working in the abolitionist movement—the movement to abolish slavery and to win freedom and equality for African Americans. Both the ideas they advocated and the political experience they gained inspired them to begin thinking about women's freedom and equality, as well. Although they were ridiculed and threatened by those who opposed them, these early feminists went on to work actively for women's rights as well as for the rights of black Americans.

This so-called first wave of feminism was split after the end of the Civil War. Although feminists and abolitionists sought voting rights for both women and former slaves, these issues were separated in Congress. Frederick Douglass—former slave, abolitionist, and ardent supporter of women's rights—urged the feminists to support black men's right to vote, with the understanding that, when that was won, the abolitionist-feminist coalition would go on to press for votes for women. Feminist Lucy Stone agreed with Douglass—but few other feminists did. A voting rights amendment enfranchising former male slaves was passed, and the powerful alliance of feminists and abolitionists was broken. Although women might have been able to win the vote earlier had the alliance remained in place, they would now have to work for this right for close to another 60 years.

After voting rights were finally won, the organized women's movement declined in the United States, although prejudice and discrimination against women still existed. Then, in the early 1970s, the so-called second wave of feminism was born. Once again, feminists who had been working in the civil rights movement to win equality for African Americans were inspired to look at their own situations, as well. They began a variety of organizations and engaged in a huge amount of scholarly and political work that explored every conceivable aspect of prejudice against women, from discrimination in employment to attitudes about sexuality.

Meanwhile, the labor market was undergoing a profound change. From a relatively small percentage of the U.S. workforce, women's participation was rapidly increasing to close to 50%. This change transformed both men's and women's ideas of who women were and what they were capable of. From the old idea of "a woman's place was in the home," people were coming to accept a new image of women active in the public sphere; the work world; the political arena; and the fields of sports, entertainment, journalism, and religion. Because they now held jobs of their own, women had the leverage to make new demands on the society as a whole, as well as on individual men.

Many of the ideas raised by feminists in the 1970s—such as "equal pay for equal work," or a woman's ability to work even after having children—now seem commonplace. Many other of those early ideas still seem quite controversial. Debate over the nature and extent of prejudice against women continues, as do arguments over the various solutions proposed for ending discrimination.

Despite the enormous changes of the past 20 years, prejudice against women is still deep-seated, however. As we have seen, even adjusting for differences in education and work experience, women earn less than 70% of what men earn. Women are still overwhelmingly concentrated in a few low-paying professions and are still largely unrepresented in the higher-paying professions. In virtually every sphere, women tend to hold the jobs at the bottom of the scale, while men hold the best-paying jobs with the most responsibility. In even the underpaid female field of day care, for example, men are more likely to be the heads of day care centers while women work as teachers or aides.

Although women have made enormous strides in the political field, they still hold much less than 50% of the political offices at any governmental level. As of 1993, there were six women senators and only a handful of women in the House of Representatives. Although there are occasional women chosen for cabinet posts and Sandra Day O'Connor now serves as the first woman Supreme Court justice, women are grossly underrepresented in both federal and state government.

Yet in other ways, the women's movement has changed the climate of opinion about women and men, bringing to national attention problems like sexual harassment, violence against women, and comparable worth—problems that did not even have a name 20 years ago. Although many types of discrimination still exist, prejudice against women is no longer thought of as an inevitable fact of life but as a problem to be debated and, eventually, solved.

4

Prejudice Against Homosexuals

A Controversial Topic

Of all the different types of prejudice and discrimination, prejudice against homosexuals—people who have sexual or romantic relationships with people of the same sex as themselves—is perhaps the most controversial. That's because people in the United States hold a wide range of views about homosexuality. Some consider it simply as another way of life. Others consider it a "sickness" or a psychological problem. Still others hold that it is sinful or contrary to the principles of religion.

Likewise, there is sharp disagreement over the issue of how people become homosexual. Some people view it as a completely free choice, in more or less the same way that deciding whether to date a particular man or a particular woman is a free choice. Other people see it as something that a person is "born with," as a person is born with blue eyes or brown hair. Still other people see homosexuality as the result of a person's upbringing, strongly influenced by the type of parents a child had and by how the parents behaved.

How a person comes to act on homosexual feelings is yet another controversial topic. Some people see the expression of these feelings as natural, in exactly the same way that having sexual feelings for the opposite sex is considered natural at a certain age. To people of this opinion, coming to act on homosexual feelings is a healthy kind of self-expression. According to this way of thinking, the only barrier to acting on homosexual feelings is the intense disapproval that many people are likely to experience from friends and family. If, however, a person is willing to disregard other people's reactions and be true to himself or herself, he or she can find a happy relationship with a person of the same sex.

Other people hold different views. They see homosexual relationships as "giving in to weakness" or even to sinful impulses. Or they think of homosexual relationships as coerced, with an older man or woman "recruiting" or "influencing" a young person to make an unhealthy choice.

There's even controversy about exactly who experiences homosexual feelings. Some people believe that we all experience a range of sexual feelings for a variety of people, particularly during the teenage years, when adult sexuality is just beginning to develop. Many factors may go into our choices about how or whether we act on those feelings, but the range itself is common to most people. In this view, there is no rigid line dividing "gay" from "straight," since many of us have occasional sexual reactions to people of both sexes, whether or not we act on those reactions.

Other people believe that these rigid lines do exist. In this view, anyone who experiences any feeling for someone of the same sex is automatically a homosexual. This way of thinking makes it quite threatening to suggest that a person might have occasional sexual feelings for people of the same sex, particularly if that person is very concerned with "proving" to self and others that he or she is not gay.

These controversies go beyond the actual question of whom a person chooses to have romantic relationships with and into the whole area of being a "real man" or a "real woman." If people think there is something wrong with being gay and are afraid that a particular feeling means that they themselves actually *are* gay, they will have a deep concern with "acting straight." They will also be eager to identify "gay" and "straight" behavior in others, so that they can draw a rigid line between themselves, the "healthy" straight people, and the others, the "sick" gay people. Thus a boy who likes to cook might worry that this somehow makes him gay—or he might worry that others would think that he was gay. He might be concerned with hiding or suppressing his own feelings about cooking, and as a result, be especially critical of other guys who like to cook. Likewise, a girl who acts strong and assertive or who enjoys the company of her girlfriends might worry about being labeled as a lesbian. If she is worried enough about this label, she might go even further and call other strong girls or close girlfriends lesbians. The question of being gay or straight has gone far beyond the actual choice of whom to be romantic with and into the area of a person's entire identity.

It isn't easy sorting through these controversial questions, particularly if you are also asking yourself questions about your own identity. However, the more clearly you are able to think about these issues, the more comfortable you can be with your own choices—and with those of others. You can learn to be at ease with your own range of feelings, likes, and dislikes and to have the freedom to behave in whatever way works best for you—and you can free yourself of stereotypes and prejudices about the behavior and actions of others.

Myths and Stereotypes

There are many myths and stereotypes about gay people, myths so common that many people have come to accept them as true. Check your own awareness about this subject with the following true-false test. Keep a record of your answers on a separate sheet of paper. Then compare them to the answers below. Did you know more or less than you thought you did?

Awareness Test on Homosexuality

____ 1. Most people become gay when an older homosexual "recruits" them or forces them to have homosexual sex.

____ 2. Most child molesters are gay.

____ 3. You can always tell a gay person by how he or she looks and acts.

____ 4. Most gay people are white.

____ 5. Gay people tend to come from more privileged backgrounds; people whose parents had to work hard for a living rarely if ever turn out to be homosexual.

____ 6. Most gay men work in fields such as dress design, dance, and interior decoration; few if any gay men are police officers, welders, construction workers, or sports figures.

____ 7. Most gay women are extremely masculine in appearance.

____ 8. People become gay because of bad experiences with people of the opposite sex, so if a gay person has a good heterosexual experience, he or she will "convert" to being straight.

____ 9. Gay people are only found in developed industrialized countries, like the United States, where they live mainly in the cities; there are no gay people in such places as African villages or rural Ireland.

____ 10. All religions, worldwide, agree that homosexuality is a sin.

____ 11. Gay people cannot have long-term, monogamous relationships.

____ 12. Only gay people can get acquired immune deficiency syndrome (the condition known as AIDS).

____ 13. Gay people are not capable of having sexual or romantic relationships with people of the opposite sex; therefore, if someone is married or has children, he or she cannot be gay.

___ 14. Gay people are essentially frivolous, living on the fringes of society and contributing very little.

___ 15. Only a very tiny minority, less than 3% of the population, can be considered gay.

How many of the statements above do you think are true? Does it surprise you to learn that every one of them is false?

1. Most people become gay when an older homosexual "recruits" them or forces them to have homosexual sex.—False. As we have said, there is a great deal of debate among psychologists and among gay people themselves over when, how, and why people become homosexual. No one knows for sure whether this is an inborn choice or the result of early childhood experiences. In either case, however, most scientists agree that a person's sexuality is formed by the time he or she becomes a teenager. Experiences at this age may affect how a person feels about sex, about himself or herself, or even how a person feels toward men and women in general. But they are very unlikely to affect the choice of being homosexual or heterosexual. Even if a person were forced or seduced into a homosexual relationship, this would not "turn" him or her into a homosexual, any more than forcing or seducing a gay person into a heterosexual relationship would "turn that person straight."

2. Most child molesters are gay.—False. According to Gabrielle I. Edwards in *Coping with Discrimination*, some 90% of all child molesters—people who have sexual contact with children—are straight. The vast majority of child molesters are straight men—men who may otherwise have sexual relationships with adult women.

Men who sexually abuse children may choose to abuse either boys or girls. Some statistics show that one girl in four and one boy in six has been sexually molested in some way—by direct sexual contact; by some other kind of inappropriate touching or kissing; by being watched while undressing, bathing, or using the bathroom, or being forced to watch someone else performing these activities; or by being spoken to or teased in a sexually inappropriate way. (If you or someone you know is being or has been sexually abused, be sure to tell an adult you can trust or call a hot line or social service agency in order to get help in stopping the situation and dealing with its aftereffects. Chapter 7 lists some agencies and hot lines that can help.) However, whether the sexually abusive adults are male or female, and whether they are abusing children of the same sex or the opposite sex as themselves, these adults are almost never homosexual. They frequently have ongoing sexual relationships or even marriages with other heterosexual adults and usually have no history of adult sexual relations with members of the same sex.

That's because much of sexual abuse and child molesting is not about sexuality so much as it as about power. An adult who forces sexual contact upon a child may be far less interested in the sexual aspect of the relationship than with proving that he or she is powerful. Thus the adult may choose one sex to have sexual relations with and another sex with which to express his or her power.

Perhaps the myth of the homosexual child abuser has its roots in the fears and misunderstandings that surround the issue of sexual abuse in general. For many years, society was unwilling to recognize that otherwise "normal" people were forcing sexual contact upon children, often children who were related to them or who otherwise were in positions of trust or dependence upon them. To hide this uncomfortable truth, many myths were created to demonstrate how different sexual abusers were from everyone else. People's discomfort with both sexual abuse and homosexuality came together to create the myth of the homosexual child abuser.

3. You can always tell a gay person by how he or she looks and acts.—False. Perhaps the most dramatic dem-

onstration of this statement's falsehood came with the reve-
lation that movie star Rock Hudson was gay. For years, Rock
Hudson had been the symbol of the romantic male hero. He
had played sexy, romantic leading roles opposite female
movie stars to the acclaim and applause of millions of
moviegoers throughout America. None of the people who
had watched him in the movies and on television talk shows
ever had the least suspicion that in his private life, Hudson
preferred relationships with men.

The myth that most gay people are easy to recognize
includes some very specific stereotypes about how gay
people act. How many of the following stereotypes do you
recognize?

Common Stereotypes About Gay Men:
- act effeminate; that is, "sissy" or "swishy"
- are preoccupied with how they look and dress
- lisp or talk in an affected way
- have limp wrists
- are weak, timid, and fearful

Common Stereotypes About Gay Women:
- swagger and act "tough"
- are muscular or fat
- dress in jeans, leather, or other "masculine" clothes
- have short hair or hair pulled back tightly
- are loud, pushy, and hostile toward men

Of course, some gay people do fit these stereotypes—although some straight people may also fit them, or some
aspect of them. According to the Institute for Sex Research,
some 15% of gay men and 5% of lesbian women are easily
recognizable by most people. These are most likely the men
and women who do fit the common stereotypes, or those
who in other ways "advertise" their sexual choices by certain
types of behavior.

The rest of the gay population—that is, the vast majority—
are "just like everybody else," except for one detail—whom
they choose to relate to romantically. Of course, whom a

person goes out with might tell you a lot about that person—
but that's true for everybody.

4. Most gay people are white.—False. Most scientists
agree that gay people are evenly distributed across all racial
and cultural groups. Gay people in some groups may be
more visible, but the same proportion of gay people seems
to exist within all races and ethnic types.

**5. Gay people tend to come from more privileged
backgrounds; people whose parents had to work hard
for a living rarely if ever turn out to be homosexual.—
False.** One of the strongest myths about homosexuality has
been the association of it with rich or upper-class people.
There are many reasons for this myth, one of which is no
doubt that wealthy homosexuals were certainly more visible
than those from among working people. Precisely because
they did have money, wealthy homosexuals could afford to
lead more obviously unconventional lives. And, as rich
people, they were more likely to be in the public eye. Thus
the "scandalous" homosexual affairs of high society would
be better known to most people of all classes than the more
hidden homosexual activity at, say, a waterfront bar.

Likewise, gay people from the upper classes were more
likely to be writers and artists than working-class gay people.
Thus they could write stories and poems and create plays
and films about their relationships. Their money and education gave them both the freedom and the opportunity to be
in the public eye, whereas few working-class people, gay or
straight, had that opportunity.

In recent years, historians, sociologists, and researchers
have become more interested in gay activity in all walks of
life. Their research shows that upper-class gay people may
be more visible, but that homosexual feelings and activity
exist among all types of people regardless of income.

**6. Most gay men work in fields such as dress design,
dance, and interior decoration; few if any gay men are
police officers, welders, construction workers, or
sports figures.—False.** Once again, we are dealing with

the difference between appearance and reality. Because it has become more acceptable for a man to be gay in certain fields, gay men in those fields are quite visible. In other fields, homosexuality is considered far less acceptable, so gay men in those fields are far more likely to hide their sexual choices. Gay men work in all sorts of professions, a fact that is becoming ever more clear as society's tolerance of homosexuality increases and gay men are becoming more willing to reveal their sexual choices.

7. Most gay women are extremely masculine in appearance.—False. This stereotype goes back to the one we discussed earlier: that most gay people are easily recognizable as gay. As we saw, only about 5% of gay women are recognizable in that way, however. Among the other 95%, there is the same range of appearance that can be found in all women.

In many ways, the stigma of being a lesbian is even greater than that of being a gay man, so it is difficult to sort out rumors from fact about which top models and Hollywood actresses actually have lesbian relationships. Just as the handsome, manly Rock Hudson turned out to be gay, however, it is likely that some ultra-feminine female star will later turn out to have been sexually involved with women.

8. People become gay because of bad experiences with people of the opposite sex, so if a gay person has a good heterosexual experience, he or she will "convert" to being straight.—False. As we have seen, actual sexual experiences seem to play very little part in whether a person becomes gay or straight. Since bad sexual experiences don't "cause" homosexuality, good sexual experiences are not likely to change it.

It is true that sometimes people have sexual relationships with people of one sex, then later choose a partner of a different sex. These choices, however, seem to be driven by other factors. Furthermore, they may go in either direction: a woman who has been married for several years may finally choose a homosexual relationship, just as a woman who has spent several years in a lesbian relationship may later establish a sexual connection with a man. Likewise, a man who has been married or otherwise involved with women may decide that he prefers male sexual partners. The least likely switch involves men who have been almost exclusively involved with other men; rarely, if ever, do they go on to establish lasting sexual relationships with women.

9. Gay people are only found in developed industrialized countries, like the United States, where they live in the cities; there are no gay people in African villages or rural Ireland.—False. As we have seen, researchers now believe that gay people are fairly evenly distributed over all racial groups, all classes, and all nationalities. What varies is not people's interest in homosexual relationships but the tolerance of the society, which affects how these relationships may be expressed. Certainly there are some societies that are far less tolerant of homosexuality than the United States, just as there are some societies that are far more tolerant of it. This may mean that in some societies, more gay people live without sexual relationships or without an awareness of their own sexuality, since they have been taught to believe that their feelings are "wrong," "unnatural," or have no place. It may also mean that gay people have close ties to people of the same sex without recognizing that they have sexual feelings for them, or without recognizing that their actions with these people are in fact quite sexual. However, there are many societies in which sexual relationships among people of the same sex are recognized and tolerated, as demonstrated by Margaret Mead's studies of the South Sea Islands of Samoa or Audre Lorde's research into traditional villages in Africa.

10. All religions, worldwide, agree that homosexuality is a sin.—False. Certainly three of the world's major religions—Judaism, Christianity, and Islam—consider homosexuality a sin, though the seriousness of the sin has varied greatly over the centuries. But as we just saw, there are many societies in which homosexuality is tolerated or accepted, and the religions of those societies are often equally tolerant.

11. Gay people cannot have long-term, monogamous relationships.—False. Another myth about gay relationships is that the sex is the most important thing about them. Whereas straight relationships are seen as involving many dimensions—emotional, spiritual, intellectual, as well as sexual—gay relationships are stereotyped as purely physical encounters. However, many gay relationships last as long as or longer than many marriages, through years of hardship and difficulty as well as times of pleasure and ease. The recent movie *Longtime Companion* focused on the devotion of longtime gay male couples, one of whom nursed the other through a prolonged and debilitating illness. The relationships portrayed in that movie certainly went beyond brief sexual encounters.

12. Only gay people can get acquired immune deficiency syndrome (the condition known as AIDS).— False. AIDS is caused by a virus that lives in blood and semen and is transmitted when a person's blood or semen comes into contact with another person's bloodstream. This transmission can take place during homosexual sex, heterosexual sex, blood transfusions, or the sharing of needles for injections. A person's sexual preference has nothing to do with his or her ability to contract or transmit AIDS—a person's *behavior* is what makes the difference. And the behaviors that transmit AIDS include anal, vaginal, and oral sex, all of which are practiced by people of all sexual preferences.[1]

13. Gay people are not capable of having sexual or romantic relationships with people of the opposite sex; therefore, if someone is married or has children, he or she cannot be gay.—False. Many gay people are capable of having sexual relationships with people of both sexes; they simply prefer one sex to another. Some people,

---

[1] Safer practices for people of all sexual preferences include using a condom during anal or vaginal sex and avoiding the swallowing of a man's sexual fluids or a woman's menstrual blood, as well as never sharing needles under any circumstances. See chapter 7 for agencies that can provide more information on AIDS.

known as *bisexuals*, seem to prefer both sexes equally and may have sexual histories that include long-term relationships with people of both sexes. Other people may wish to have heterosexual relationships for a variety of reasons, particularly to avoid the stigma of being labeled as "gay." They may marry and even have children with a partner of the opposite sex, while remaining more emotionally attached to or sexually interested in people of the same sex. In some cases, people have ignored or repressed their true sexual feelings for many years, even throughout a marriage, until they are finally able to make another kind of choice.

14. Gay people are essentially frivolous, living on the fringes of society and contributing very little.—False. This stereotype indicates the deep prejudice that many people have against gay people, which includes the wish to deny the genuine accomplishments of people who happened to be gay. The stereotype also indicates the extent to which gay people have often felt the need to hide their sexuality, in order to avoid the disapproval of those around them. Thus a person might become well known as a writer, artist, scientist, or political leader and seek to hide his or her sexual preference.

Here is a list of just some of the people throughout history whom scholars now believe to have been gay: 19th-century British writer Oscar Wilde; 20th-century American writer Gertrude Stein; Harlem Renaissance writer Langston Hughes; 4th century, B.C. emperor and world leader Alexander the Great; the ancient Greek philosopher Plato; Renaissance playwright Christopher Marlowe; 19th-century American poet Walt Whitman; late-19th-century French writer Marcel Proust; 20th-century American writers Willa Cather and Tennessee Williams. Contemporary gay figures include poet Adrienne Rich, Massachusetts Congressman Barney Frank, San Francisco City Councilor Harry Britt, and tennis player Martina Navratilova.

15. Only a very tiny minority, less than 3% of the population, can be considered gay.—False. According to the Kinsey Report, the major study of U.S. sexual practices, some 10% of the population is gay. Most researchers believe that this figure is probably valid for societies and cultural groups around the world and throughout history, although the ways that the gay population acts and sees itself has varied a great deal.

What this 10% figure means is that in all likelihood, you know several people who are gay—adults, other teenagers, relatives, friends. You may or may not be aware of who they are, but you are almost certainly acquainted with them.

Discrimination and Violence Against Gay People

So far, we have been talking about homosexuality primarily in terms of the stereotypes that people have about it. But, as we have seen, stereotypes usually indicate that some other kind of discrimination is also being practiced.

Discrimination against gay people takes a variety of forms. Unlike members of other groups, gay people may be able to hide their identities, in order to avoid prejudice. This becomes a deep form of discrimination in itself. Gay people may feel that they cannot have ongoing romantic relationships, for fear of their identity being discovered. They may feel the need to hide these relationships or even to lie and pretend that they are dating people of the opposite sex. They may worry that if their true identities were known, they would have difficulty renting apartments, keeping jobs, winning promotions, or being accepted in various social situations. They may also be concerned about acceptance by their families.

Discrimination in employment and housing are against federal law for most other groups—but not for gay people. Although some cities and institutions have regulations prohibiting discrimination on the basis of sexual preference, many do not. Thus an employer may be within his or her legal rights to say, "Now that I have this information about your private life, I prefer not to work with you." Likewise a landlord may refuse to rent to a gay couple in many cities or threaten the couple with eviction if the nature of their relationship becomes apparent.

Gay people also face discrimination in the cultural arena. There are virtually no gay characters in popular television shows or films, and those that do appear are often marked by stereotyping. Advertising, journalism, and most entertainment tend to simply ignore the fact that gay people exist.

Historically, the medical and psychiatric professions were biased against gay people, considering their life-style and practices "unnatural" and "unhealthy" by definition. Over the years, however, these attitudes have changed. Several years ago, the American Psychiatric Association officially took homosexuality off its list of mental health problems, certifying that being homosexual was not in itself a cause for psychiatric treatment.

Religious groups also may discriminate against gay people. Most Christian, Jewish, and Islamic groups do not accept gay religious leaders, although their attitudes toward gay members may vary. Some groups, such as the Catholic organization "Dignity" and the Episcopal group "Integrity" were founded specifically to give religious gay people a home within their churches. Although many gay leaders have criticized the Catholic Church's stand on homosexuality, the National Federation of Priests' Councils has come out in support of gay Catholics. Likewise, there are some gay temples and organizations to support Jewish gay people.

An even more serious result of prejudice against gay people is outright violence. Particularly as gay people have been willing to be more open about their identities, they have faced beatings and other violent incidents from gangs of young people who frequently seek out gay bars or gay neighborhoods, looking for people to harass. Gay rights groups have claimed that police are often unsympathetic to their complaints or even that police themselves tend to treat gay citizens with violence.

Gay Rights and the Law

Just as the civil rights movement of the 1950s and 1960s inspired protest among Native Americans and Hispanic Americans, so did it encourage gay people to organize on their own behalf as well. Their movement began in a now-famous incident in 1969, when New York City police raided Stonewall, a Greenwich Village bar that was a center of gay activity. The riots that ensued reflected gay people's frustration with police harassment—and with a society in which they felt the need to hide their identities in order to avoid the other types of harassment we have described.

The Stonewall riots inspired a nationwide movement to pass gay rights legislation—city and state laws guaranteeing that there will be no discrimination in housing, employment, or government services on the basis of sexual preference. In the late 1960s and early 1970s, many cities passed such bills. At the same time, states that had outlawed certain types of behavior were often induced to take those laws off the books.

Then, in 1976, a backlash, or reaction, began. The U.S. Supreme Court upheld a lower court's ruling that people could in fact be prosecuted and jailed for homosexual activity carried on between consenting adults in the privacy of their own homes. Even though such laws were rarely if ever enforced, gay people felt that such laws represented an invasion of privacy for all people. This was particularly true since many states simply had laws against sodomy—including oral or anal sex involving a penis—which might be practiced by either homosexual or heterosexual couples. Although 22 states have repealed all laws against sexual behavior between consenting adults, many other states still have laws against sodomy and other practices on the books.

The year 1976 also saw the beginning of an organized movement specifically against gay rights. Singer Anita Bryant led a group seeking to repeal the gay rights law that had been passed in Florida's Dade County. In 1977, she was successful. In 1978, a Baptist minister in St. Paul, Minnesota, had similar success in repealing that city's gay rights ordinance. Gay people began to fear that the gains they had made throughout the early 1970s would soon be reversed.

Since that time, progress towards gay rights has been mixed. On the one hand, there has been ever greater tolerance of gay participation in a variety of fields, particularly politics, with the election of openly gay candidates such as San Francisco City Councilor Harry Britt and Massachusetts Congressman Barney Frank. Likewise, there has been a greater presence of nonstereotypical gays on television and in the movies, as well as several films and television movies specifically designed to give a sympathetic portrait of gay characters.

On the other hand, particularly with the spread of AIDS, there has been an increase in violence against gay people. And anti-gay groups continue to organize against gay rights. Periodically, states like California and Oklahoma see movements to bar gay people from teaching positions (movements opposed by all the major teachers' unions). Politicians feel free to make anti-gay statements the cornerstone of their campaigns. When in 1984 New York City's Mayor Ed Koch required equal opportunity employment for gay people among all groups doing business with the city, Catholic, Jewish, and Protestant groups refused. They claimed that equal rights for gay employees in their child care and social service agencies would violate their religious teachings.

Despite the backlash, gay rights groups continue to press for new legal and social victories. In some cities, laws have been passed allowing unmarried people to claim "spousal rights"—that is, the same rights that a husband or wife would have for family insurance and other employee benefits.

While such laws benefit unmarried straight couples as well as gay couples, they are a clear step forward for society's recognition of the legitimacy of gay relationships.

It isn't clear what the future holds for the gay rights movement. Both the backlash against gay rights and the movement for gay rights seem to have strengthened—and both movements seem determined to continue. Despite setbacks, however, it seems that the United States is definitely moving toward a greater tolerance of gay people, and toward the belief that prejudice of all types is wrong.

Anti-Gay Feeling and Straight People

Prejudice of all kinds hurts everyone—those who promote prejudice as well as those who are its targets. This is especially clear with prejudice against gay people. Deciding that a certain way of life is wrong, and then building up all sorts of myths and stereotypes about that life, limits everyone's options.

For example, if a boy is particularly worried about being or seeming gay, he may deny himself the fun of certain kinds of activities, like cooking, dance, or design. He may hold back on his closeness with other guys, denying himself certain aspects of friendship or sharing because of his fear. He may also avoid other boys who are more willing to break the stereotypes, denying himself *their* friendship, either because they are gay or because they seem gay. Whether or not a boy is gay, if being gay seems wrong or dangerous, the boy may limit himself in all sorts of ways out of fear of being or seeming gay.

Likewise, girls worried about being or looking like lesbians may feel the need to restrict themselves—from sports, from being assertive, from dressing casually or not wearing makeup, from having close relationships with other girls. The fear of being labeled a lesbian may keep a girl from exploring all sorts of ways of being and feeling that would help her find out more about herself and the things she most enjoys.

On the other hand, if many types of behavior and feelings are tolerated, both gay and straight people are more free to explore their feelings and identities, in romance as well as in all other ways. Overcoming prejudice and discrimination is thus in everybody's best interest.

5

Prejudice Against the Aged and the Handicapped

A Type of Prejudice That Affects Us All

Most of the prejudice we've examined so far affects groups that you have to be born into or to choose consciously. However, some groups are neither chosen nor assigned from birth. If we are lucky, we will all live to be old someday. And any of us, no matter how able-bodied at the moment, might become handicapped by an accident or a disease. Thus prejudice against the aged and the handicapped potentially affects every one of us.[1]

Perhaps the very awareness of this fact contributes to the prejudice against these two groups. After all, the idea that someday a person might face the loss of a sense or a part of the body is an extremely uncomfortable notion. So is the idea that someday we will be much closer to death than we are now. To some, insisting that "those people" are very different from us, that "they" are weak and useless while "we" are strong and powerful may seem like a way of coping with the discomfort.

Thus young or "temporarily able-bodied" people may develop negative stereotypes about the aged and the handicapped in order to comfort themselves. The problem with this way of coping, of course, is that it's based on an untruth. As we have seen, although stereotypes may have some truth in them, they are not really accurate pictures of reality. A person who has accepted stereotypes about the aged or the handicapped in order to overcome his or her own fear of aging or of becoming disabled is basically believing in a fairy tale rather than looking directly and honestly at life.

Furthermore, relying on stereotypes doesn't really solve the problem. Even if believing the myth that the aged and the handicapped are "different" from "everybody else" does make some people feel protected from age, accident, or disease, the protection is only temporary. No matter what our age or physical condition, we all share the same risks of being human. Sooner or later, anyone might find him-

---

[1] Physical handicaps might include the loss or impairment of a sense—being completely or partially blind, deaf or hearing-impaired—or the loss or impairment of some other physical capability—such as being wheelchair-bound, needing crutches, having difficulties with motor coordination (that is, difficulty in using one's hands and arms), having a speech impediment, or some combination of these conditions. None of the handicaps discussed in this chapter include mental retardation or developmental disabilities; that is, none of the physical handicaps mentioned here means that a person has trouble thinking or using his or her mind in any way.

self or herself old or disabled, and nothing can change that fact. Since deep down, everybody knows this, distancing from the aged or the handicapped doesn't really make anyone less uncomfortable. It only puts off the day when the person really will have to face his or her discomfort.

Negative Stereotypes— and Some Falsely Positive Ones

Of course, stereotypes are not only negative. Sometimes stereotypes seem to attribute positive qualities to people, as well. Following is a list of some common stereotypes about the aged and the handicapped. Which do you recognize? Can you think of any other stereotypes held by you or by others that you know?

Some Common Stereotypes About the Elderly

- cranky
- senile (can't think clearly)
- out of touch with today's issues
- kindly
- spoil their grandchildren
- wise
- old-fashioned
- narrow-minded
- not interested in sexual relationships or romance
- happy to baby-sit young children
- "set in their ways"
- childlike
- easily frightened

Some Common Stereotypes About the Handicapped

- weak
- not interested in sexual relationships or romance
- more spiritual than others
- unusually patient
- low intelligence
- self-sacrificing, unselfish
- childlike
- timid, fearful
- handicapped in many ways (for example, the stereotype that a blind person also has difficulty moving; or that a wheelchair-bound person doesn't hear well)
- innocent
- crafty, deceitful
- dependent
- unwilling to accept any help from others
- touchy
- easily embarrassed or offended
- not interested in activities that "normal" people enjoy, such as movies, music, sports

As you can see, many of the stereotypes contradict one another. Handicapped people may be stereotyped as touchy, easily offended, and difficult to get along with— or as saintly, patient, spiritual people who spend their lives sacrificing themselves to others. The elderly may be stereotyped as cranky and intolerant or as eternally loving grandparents; as senile and incompetent or as unusually wise.

You may also have noticed that many of the stereotypes of the two groups overlap. People in both groups may be seen as timid, fearful, unintelligent, or childlike. Perhaps these images are a reflection of the fears that others have of losing some of their physical capacities, along with the fear of losing mental or emotional capacities as well.

Of course, as we have seen, some parts of stereotypes may occasionally apply to some people. Some elderly people may be cranky and old-fashioned; some handicapped people may be timid or unusually patient. And of course, these adjectives may apply to people who are not elderly or handicapped, as well. The problem with a stereotype is not that it is never true, but that it leads you to assume that you already know all you need to know about a person who is, say, elderly, or handicapped, rather than treating each person as an individual whose strengths and weaknesses are not necessarily defined by age or physical condition. Even if a person is *affected* by these qualities, many other factors go into shaping someone's personality and behavior.

Check Your Own Awareness

As we have seen, prejudice, stereotyping, and discrimination can sometimes take subtle forms. Can you spot the prejudice in the following situations?

- Carla goes to apply for a secretarial job. She takes the typing test, which proves that she can type 70 words a minute. She is familiar with all the latest computer systems, and her resume shows over 25 years of experience. The interviewer says, "We're very impressed with your background—but our company has to uphold the image of being modern and up-to-date. I'm afraid that you don't quite fit that image."
- Leroy is a new student at Washington High School. Joe, who sits next to him in history class, suggests inviting him to join a group of friends who are getting together that Friday night. Lou says, "I don't think he'd be that much fun. What could we do with a blind guy? We

couldn't go to a movie or to the basketball game. And we'll all have dates—he'd feel left out."

- José recently lost his job when the insurance company he worked for went out of business. In his old job, he was a department manager with a good work record. Now, however, he is having trouble finding another job. One company tells him, "We don't hire managers—we only promote from within. We'd have to start you at a lower salary than you were getting before—and we just don't think you'd be very happy if we did that." Another company tells him, "If we hired you, Mr. Lamb would be your supervisor—and I just don't think he'd be comfortable giving orders to someone so much older than himself."

- Alyssa is severely hearing-impaired. Although she is able to read lips and to speak to some extent, she prefers to communicate in American Sign Language, a language of gestures used by many deaf people. When she reads lips, Alyssa is able to understand only about 60% to 80% of what is said, and when she speaks, she must speak slowly and carefully. When she signs, however, she feels comfortable and fluent, able to understand everything and to express herself with ease. She asks her college professor if she can pay to bring a sign-language interpreter in to sign the lectures for her. "No," says the professor, "I think it would be too disturbing for the other students."

- Eric can get around on crutches, but he finds it much easier to use a wheelchair—it leaves his hands free, and he can move more quickly and easily. However, whenever he goes out he has to be extremely well prepared, because there is a long list of things he can't do: make a call on a public phone (too high), use some public bathrooms (too narrow), enter some public buildings (stairs and no access ramps).

- Marge has been a successful author of self-help books for many years. She has a degree in psychology and has won several honors from colleges and universities.

When she goes on a talk show to advertise her latest book, the interviewer says, "Oh, it's such a pleasure to meet you! I always think of you as everybody's favorite grandmother!"

- At her next job interview, Carla again does well on the typing test—and again fails to get the job. As she leaves, one of the other secretaries takes her aside and says, "Don't feel bad. You were interviewing to be Mr. Martin's private secretary—and he always hires the prettiest woman he can find."

- Thomas graduates in the top tenth of his law school class and looks forward to finding a place at a top law firm. He has a form of *cerebral palsy*—a disease that causes various types of paralysis—that restricts him to a wheelchair and leaves him with a slight *tremor*—or shaking—in his hands and in his speech. He interviews with several law firms in his city, but he doesn't get a single job, even though classmates who were ranked below him seem to be finding positions that they like. Thomas notices that when he meets the lawyers who will decide whether or not to hire him, they always avoid looking at his hands.

- Calvin has been a widower (someone whose wife has died) for about five years, and he's now in his early sixties. He has been invited to a dinner party at the house of a fellow professor at the college where he works. He hears her talking about the various couples who will be there and about how she is trying to find dates for the guests who will be single. "Who have you got lined up for me?" he asks. She looks at him in surprise. "You?" she says. "I didn't think you were interested in that kind of thing any more."

- One day, Leroy is having lunch with Joe, Lou, and their friends. They are having an argument, and Leroy seems to be winning. "I see what you mean," says Lou. Then Lou remembers that Leroy is blind and becomes thoroughly embarrassed. He stops talking and won't say another thing for the rest of the lunch hour, even though

Leroy doesn't seem to be upset or even to have noticed anything out of the ordinary.

As the above examples reveal, *age discrimination* has many aspects. Carla, for example, is a target of the stereotype that says that older people are old-fashioned and backwards, rather than "modern" and "up-to-date." She is also hurt by the assumption that younger women are more attractive and more pleasant to be around than older women.

José is also the target of age discrimination in employment. Many companies prefer to hire younger people who are just out of school or who have shorter work records because such employees can be paid lower salaries than older, more experienced workers. To some extent, this is an example of institutional discrimination—a policy that ends up hurting a whole group of people without any conscious thought or acknowledgment that this is what has happened. This policy is also fed by the stereotype that older people are slower, less aggressive, and generally less effective than young people.

Furthermore, José is told that he will make other people uncomfortable simply because he is old. He is told that his supervisor will not be able to view José as just another competent employee; instead, he will be disturbed by the fact that José is older than he is. Because José's age might make someone else uncomfortable, José is denied a job that he is qualified for.

Marge faces another kind of age discrimination—the stereotype that refuses to take elderly people seriously as competent professionals. This stereotype is particularly damaging to women, who, as we have seen, are often not viewed as competent professionals at any age. Older women, however, are especially vulnerable to being dismissed in this way, since they have two stereotypes to overcome—those of women and those of the elderly.

Like Carla and Marge, Calvin is a target of the assumption that older people are somehow different from younger people. Just as younger people assume that Carla would not measure up as a sexually attractive woman, or that Marge can be dismissed as a sweet old grandmother, someone has assumed that Calvin is no longer interested in dating and romance, simply because of his age. Assuming that someone is no longer a sexual person can be a way of not taking that person seriously, almost of treating him or her like a child instead of a mature adult.

Likewise, stereotypes and prejudice against the handicapped can take a wide range of forms. Leroy is hurt by others' assumptions that simply because a person is handicapped, he or she has nothing in common with anyone else, as though the handicap were such an important thing that it affected every single other aspect of the person's interests and personality. Thus Leroy's classmates assume that he won't be interested in movies or sports, just because he is blind. In fact, many blind people attend movies, sporting events, and other forms of entertainment that can be heard as well as seen.

Leroy's classmates also assume that because Leroy is blind, he has no interest in dating or could not successfully find a date. Again, it's as though they see Leroy's handicap as so enormous that it overshadows every other thing about him, blotting out all the ways in which he is both an individual and "just another guy."

Both Leroy and Thomas experience the unpleasant effects of others' nervousness about *their* handicaps. Like most blind people, Leroy is perfectly comfortable with common expressions like "I see what you mean"—but his classmate Lou may avoid Leroy in the future because of his *own* discomfort with using these words around a blind person. Likewise, Thomas has come to terms with his own handicap and has achieved a high degree of success as a law student. Because of other people's discomfort with his handicap, however, he may be denied the chance to take a job that he could do very well.

Alyssa and Eric experience a different type of difficulty: the denial of services that would allow them to take part in society as a whole. Alyssa is capable of attending college courses but would benefit from a sign-language translator. Eric is mobile but requires some accommodation to the fact that he is in a wheelchair. In a sense, the lack of these services is a form of institutional discrimination; simply by *not* providing them, society is denying itself the full participation of people like Eric and Alyssa. This sets up a vicious cycle: By not providing services, society helps to segregate handicapped people from everyone else; segregating them reinforces the idea that they really are completely "different," as well as incapable of taking a full and active part in society.

Discrimination and the Law

For many years, discrimination against the aged and the handicapped was so commonly accepted that it was not even seen as discrimination. The idea that "Of *course* an older person isn't right for that job" or "We would never hire her—she's blind!" was not viewed as prejudice but as a simple recognition of reality.

Then the civil rights movement of the 1950s and 1960s raised the issues of equality, prejudice, and discrimination in a new way. Suddenly, Americans were being told that the federal government had a responsibility to guarantee equal opportunity and protection from discrimination to all its citizens, regardless of race or color.

As we have seen, African Americans' push for equality set off similar movements among other cultural groups, and among women. It sparked similar social activism among the elderly and the handicapped.

Age discrimination in employment is now against federal law. Just as it is no longer legal to advertise for a member of a particular racial group or of a particular gender to do a job, so it is no longer legal to ask for "bright young person" or to specify "person in early twenties wanted." Nor is it legal to refuse to hire someone simply on the grounds of age. If a person believes that he or she has been the target of age discrimination, he or she can bring suit against the employer.

Of course, age discrimination is extremely difficult to prove. Now that it is illegal, few employers will come right out and say, "We are looking for a younger person." Interviewers are not allowed to ask a person's age directly. A person who believes that age discrimination has been practiced must look for more subtle clues—such as the remarks that Carla's interviewer made about "our company's image," or José's interviewer's suggestion that "You're used to a higher salary—you wouldn't be happy here." The employer may not even be aware that he or she is in fact practicing age discrimination; he or she may simply feel that every older person who interviews for a job just "happens" not to fit the job description.

In order to combat both age discrimination and other forms of prejudice against the elderly, many older people formed a group known as the Gray Panthers. This group took its name from the African-American group known as the Black Panthers. The Gray Panthers work against age discrimination and for the rights of the aged in a variety of ways, including pushing for a national health care plan, increases in Social Security payments, and other services for senior citizens.

Just as the civil rights movement sparked a political movement of the elderly, so did it inspire a variety of handicapped rights' movements concerned both with guaranteeing legal rights to the handicapped and with overcoming more subtle prejudices. One major victory of this movement was the passage of the federal Public Law 94-142, which guarantees all children the right to a free and appropriate education, regardless of physical or mental handicap. Before this law, school systems might say that they were simply not equipped to teach the blind, the deaf, or the orthopedically handicapped. After the law was passed, school systems had to serve these children. The law also encouraged "mainstreaming"—that is, integrating handicapped children into the "mainstream" of education wherever possible, rather than segregating them into special classes in subjects where they were perfectly able to join the other children.

Another federal law, PL 93-112, forbids discrimination against the handicapped by the federal government, requiring equal access to federal buildings and services or to buildings supported by federal money. Wheelchair ramps, elevators, and other equal-access measures had to be made available so that handicapped people could join their neighbors at the voting booth, the town council meeting—or at the concert in the federally funded arts complex.

The Rehabilitation Act of 1973 went a step further in defending handicapped rights: It made it illegal to discriminate against a person solely on the basis of handicap. That is, a person cannot be denied a job on the basis of a handicap if that handicap does not prevent him or her from doing the job.

Of course, as with age discrimination, prejudice against people with handicaps is extremely difficult to prove. Both increased legal protection and changes in social attitudes will be necessary to end this type of prejudice. Fortunately, each improvement in employment or services helps bring more handicapped people into the rest of society, where others can learn to overcome their own discomforts, prejudices, and fears. These changing attitudes should, in turn, help build more support for further changes in policy and law.

6

Coping with Prejudice

Now that we have examined many different kinds of prejudice, what do we do next? Exploring so much discrimination and unfairness, so many deep-seated stereotypes, can be upsetting, frightening, maddening, painful, or confusing. In order not to feel overwhelmed by what we have learned, we have to start finding ways of coping with prejudice.

Individual Ways of Coping

Whether you are the target of prejudice, someone who holds prejudices, or both, or just someone who is concerned about prejudice in society, there is a lot you can do to cope with prejudice as an individual. Here is a brief list of various ideas. Some may appeal to you; some may not; some may seem appealing, but impossible. Perhaps the ideas on this list will be just the notions that will work for you; perhaps they will inspire you to come up with new ways of coping that will work better than these. Can you think of any that could be added to the list?

Some Personal Ways of Coping With Prejudice

- Read more about a particular group: its history and political movements, or possibly some of the writings that its political leaders have produced.
- Read a novel or see a movie focusing on a particular group.
- Attend a political meeting or a cultural event sponsored by a group.
- Make a resolution that whenever anyone expresses a remark that you consider prejudiced, you will speak up in some way.
- Take a look at the activities you do regularly: sports, drama, the school paper, clubs, hanging out with friends, going to school events. Is there some way you could broaden the range of who participates in these activities?
- Take a look at conditions in your school. Could you and your classmates stand to learn more about one of the groups discussed in this book? Talk to a social studies teacher about inviting a guest speaker, or talk to an English teacher about reading a book or watching a film that deals with prejudice, with another culture, or with one of the issues discussed in this book. Alone or with other students, organize a "Tolerance Day" or teach-in to look more closely at some of the issues that interest you.

Legal Ways of Coping

Traditionally, laws and the courts have been two important tools used to cope with prejudice. Groups such as the National Association for the Advancement of Colored People (NAACP) spent years challenging laws and court decisions that supported segregation of African Americans. Groups such as the National Organization for Women

(NOW) continue to lobby Congress for legislation funding day-care centers or making it easier for women to protect their legal rights.

If this course of action appeals to you, you might want to do some research into the laws of your community to see how they affect the issues discussed in this book. A local political action group might already be lobbying or petitioning for changes to be made. Chapter 7 lists some organizations that work to combat certain types of discrimination. Supporting or volunteering to do work for one of these groups might appeal to you as a way to work against prejudice.

Political Means of Coping

One excellent way of coping with prejudice is to elect political candidates who will oppose discrimination in all its forms. You might explore the political activity in your community to see whether any organizations are supporting candidates whom you believe will help combat prejudice and fight discrimination.

Political action can also take the form of demonstrations, teach-ins, forums, or other public events designed to draw attention to a bad situation and encourage people to change it. Often these actions are combined with petitions or letter-writing campaigns to the media or to political leaders. You and your classmates may wish to take some kind of action of this type, or you may find an organization in your community that you can work with.

However you respond to prejudice and discrimination, the first step is to be aware of the problem. The second step is to remember the enormous difference that people have made throughout history, simply by taking action, alone and with others. If you continue to educate yourself, to be aware, and to be committed to doing what you believe to be right, you can both cope with prejudice and begin to overcome it.

7

Where to Find Help

The organizations and hot lines listed below provide information and, in some cases, assistance with various types of discrimination discussed in this book. Some of these organizations also offer work to volunteers who want to aid efforts to combat prejudice and discrimination.

The Aging

The following organizations provide information and referrals for the aging:

American Association of Retired Persons (AARP)
1-800-453-5800

Center for the Study of Aging
706 Madison Avenue
Albany, NY 12208
518-465-6927

The Gray Panthers
15 West 65th Street
New York, NY 10023
212-799-7572

The National Council on the Aging, Inc.
1-800-424-9046

Civil Liberties and Human Rights

The following organizations provide information, referrals, and, in some cases, legal assistance in all areas of discrimination:

American Civil Liberties Union (ACLU)
132 West 43rd Street
New York, NY 10036
212-944-9800

Civil Rights Division, Department of Justice
10th Street & Constitution Avenue NW
Washington, DC 20530
202-514-2000

International League for Human Rights
432 Park Avenue South
New York, NY 10016
212-684-1221

National Legal Center for the Public Interest
1000 16th Street NW
Washington, DC 20036
202-296-1683

Religious Coalition for Abortion Rights
100 Maryland Avenue NE
Washington, DC 20002
202-543-7032

U.S. Commission on Civil Rights
624 9th Street NW
Washington, DC 20415
202-376-8177

The Handicapped/ Physically Challenged

The following organizations provide resources and referrals for the physically challenged and disabled.

American Council of the Blind
1-800-424-8666

American Foundation for the Blind
15 West 16th Street
New York, NY 10011
1-800-232-5463
212-620-2000 (New York City only)

Arts Carousel/Arts with the Handicapped Foundation
Box 342
Station P
Toronto, Ontario M5S 2S8
An organization devoted to improving the quality of life of the handicapped through creative arts.

Association for Children and Adults with Learning
  Disabilities
412-341-1515

Canadian Council of the Blind
405-396 Cooper Street
Ottawa, Ontario K2P 2H7
613-567-0311

Canadian Hearing Society
Information Services Dept.
271 Spadina Road
Toronto, Ontario M5R 2V3
416-964-9595

Office of Civil Rights
1-800-368-1019
For friends or parents of handicapped infants denied medical care.

HEATH (Higher Education and the
    Handicapped)
1-800-544-3284

Job Accommodation Network (JAN)
1-800-526-7234

JOB (Just One Break)
373 Park Avenue South
New York, NY 10016
212-725-2500
This organization is an employment agency for the handicapped.

National Accreditation Council for Agencies Serving
    the Blind and Visually Handicapped
15 E. 40th Street
Suite 1004
New York, NY 10016
212-683-5068

National Association for the Visually
  Handicapped
22 West 21st Street
New York, NY 10010
212-889-3141

National Association of the Deaf
301-587-1788

National Information Center for Handicapped
  Children & Youth with Disabilities
P.O. Box 1492
Washington, DC 20013
703-893-6061

National Organization on Disability (NOD)
1-800-248-2253

The Homeless/The Poor

The following organizations provide information and referrals to those who feel they have been discriminated against
because they are homeless or receive public assistance.

Coalition for the Homeless
500 Eighth Avenue
New York, NY 10018
212-695-8700

National Legal Aid and Defender Association
1625 K Street NW
8th Floor
Washington, DC 20006
202-452-0620

Housing

The following organization offers information and referrals to those who feel they have been discriminated against in housing—whether because of race, sex, religion, national origin, or sexual preference.

Fair Housing and Equal Opportunity Hotline
1-800-669-9777

Physical and Sexual Abuse

The following agencies can provide information and assistance about various types of abuse mentioned in this book.

American Humane Association
63 Inverness Drive East
Englewood, CO 80112
303-792-9900
The American Humane Association protects children against neglect and abuse through a variety of community service programs.

Childhelp/International
6463 Independence Avenue
Woodland Hills, CA 91370
1-800-4-A-CHILD
Childhelp provides crisis counseling information and referrals in situations dealing with child abuse.

Society for the Prevention of Cruelty to Children
161 William Street
New York, NY 10038
212-233-5500
This organization provides referrals and counseling to families and children suffering from physical and sexual abuse.

Race, Religion, National Origin

The following organizations provide information and referrals to those who feel they have been discriminated against because of their race, religion, or national origin.

American Jewish Congress
15 East 84th Street
New York, NY 10028
212-879-4500

Anti-Defamation League of B'nai B'rith
823 U.N. Plaza
New York, NY 10017
212-490-2525

A. Philip Randolph Institute
1444 I Street NW
3rd Floor
Washington, DC 20005
202-289-2774

Provides advisory and reference services in black education, political activism, and leadership development.

Association of American Indian Affairs
245 Fifth Avenue
Room 1801
New York, NY 10016
212-689-8720

Bureau of Indian Affairs
Department of the Interior
1849 C Street NW
Washington, DC 20245
202-208-3710

Congress of Racial Equality (CORE)
30 Cooper Square
New York, NY 10001
212-598-4000

The Field Foundation
135 South La Salle
Suite 1250
Chicago, IL 60603
312-263-3211
Promotes educational programs in race relations and civil liberties.

Interchurch Center, Ecumenical Library
475 Riverside Drive
New York, NY 10115
212-870-3804

National Association for Puerto Rican Civil Rights
2134 Third Avenue
New York, NY 10037
212-996-9661

National Association for the Advancement of Colored People
   (NAACP)
144 West 125th Street
New York, NY 10027
212-666-9740

National Conference of Christians and Jews
71 Fifth Avenue
Suite 1100
New York, NY 10003
212-206-0006

National Congress of American Indians
900 Pennsylvania Avenue SE
Washington, DC 20003
202-546-9404

National Urban League
500 East 62nd Street
New York, NY 10021
212-310-9000
Promotes civil rights and civil liberties, works toward the
elimination of all discrimination.

Office of Bilingual Education & Minority Languages
   Affairs
Department of Education
400 Maryland Avenue SW
Washington, DC 20202

Sexual Discrimination

The following organizations offer information and referrals
to those who feel they have been discriminated against
because of their sex or sexual orientation.

Gay and Lesbian Advocates and Defenders (GLAD)
617-807-1700

Gay and Lesbian Alliance Against Defamation (GLAAD)
212-807-1700

National Organization for Men, Inc.
381 Park Avenue South
New York, NY 10016
212-686-6253

National Organization for Women (NOW)
15 West 18th Street
New York, NY 10011
212-807-0721

Sexually Transmitted Diseases

The following organizations can provide information on sexually transmitted diseases, including AIDS, and on safer sex practices.

Centers for Disease Control AIDS Hotline
1-800-342-2437

Centers for Disease Control STDs Hotline
1-800-227-8922

American Foundation for AIDS Research
733 Third Avenue
12th floor
New York, NY 10017
212-682-7440

CHOICE Hotline
215-592-0550

This help line answers teenagers' questions about sexually transmitted diseases, AIDS, birth control, pregnancy, and other related topics. Spanish operators available.

Gay Men's Health Crisis Hotline
212-807-6655

Planned Parenthood Federation of America
810 Seventh Avenue
New York, NY 10019
212-541-7800
This organization provides information on sexually transmitted diseases, birth control, sexuality, and family life.

INDEX

A

Abolitionist movement, 37
  women's rights movement, 73
Abuse—*See Physical abuse; Sexual abuse*
Activism
  coping through, 108
  Hispanic Americans, 45–46
  Native Americans, 33–35
Advertisements
  emphasis on appearance in, 16
Africa
  European view of, in Middle Ages, 7
  homosexuality in traditional villages in, 85
African Americans
  American Nazi party, 28
  civil rights movement, 39
  Jim Crow laws, 37–38
  Ku Klux Klan, 27–28
  legal discrimination, 2
  migration to North, 38
  police violence against in Los Angeles, 21–22
  poverty, 39–40
  right to vote, 2, 39, 73
  slavery, 35–37
  stereotypes about, 8
  women, 40
Age discrimination
  assumptions about elderly, 101–102
  examples of, 98–100
  resources for, 109–110
  sources of, 94–96
  stereotypes about, 96
AIDS
  homosexuality and, 85
  resources for, 120
  violence against homosexuals and, 91
Alexander the Great, 87
American Indian Movement (AIM), 33
American Indians—*See Native Americans*
American Nazi party, 28
American Psychiatric Association, 89
American Sign Language, 99
Anthony, Susan B., 73
Anthropologists, 9
Anti-Semitism, 53–56
Arab Americans, 56–57
Asia
  disciplining of children, 10–11
  European view of, in Middle Ages, 7
Asian Americans
  Chinese Americans, 47–51
  economic success of, 50–52
  history, 47
  immigration to U.S.
    before World War II, 47–48
    since World War II, 49–50
  Japanese Americans, 48–51
  unique position of, 46–47

B

Banks
  institutionalized discrimination in, 18
Battering, 67–68
Bensonhurst (Brooklyn, New York), 21–22
Bingham, Theodore, 53
Bisexuals, 87
Black Hills (South Dakota), 32
Blacks—*See African Americans*
Blaming the victim, 26–27
  Hispanic Americans, 44–45
Boarding schools
  Native Americans in, 34
Book publishers
  intitutionalized discrimination by, 19
Britt, Harry, 87, 91
Bryant, Anita, 91
Buffalo, destruction of, 31
Butler, Jane, 68–69

C

California
  economic success of Asian Americans in, 50–51
  emigration of Mexicans to, 42
  Native Americans in 19th century, 31
  political activism among Chicanos in, 46
Cambodia
  emigration to U.S. from, 50
Careers
  homosexuals and, 83–84
  women and, 68–69
Castro, Fidel, 41
Cather, Willa, 87
Catholic Church
  homosexuals and, 89, 91
Causes of prejudice
  cultural differences, 10–12
  economic competition, 12–15
  insecurity, 15–16
Central America
  emigration to U.S. from, 41
Cerebral palsy, 100
Chavez, Cesar, 46
Cherry, Robert, 61
Chicanos—*See Mexican Americans*
Child molesters, 80–81
Child-rearing
  women and, 62–63
Children
  cultural standards for behavior of, 11
  disciplining of, 10–11
China
  European view of, in Middle Ages, 7
Chinese Americans
  economic success and, 50–51
  immigration to U.S., 47
  labor market and, 48–49
Chinese Exclusion Act (1882), 47
Christianity
  African Americans and, 36
  homosexuality and, 85, 89
  in medieval Spain, 7
Civil liberties

resources for, 110–111
Civil Rights Act (1964)
  sexual harassment, 64
Civil rights movement
  African Americans, 39
  elderly and handicapped, 103
  gay rights and, 90
  Hispanic Americans, 46
  women's rights movement and, 73
Civil War, U.S. (1861-65), 31
Colleges and universities
  quotas for Jewish enrollment in, 54–55
Columbia University, 54–55
Columbus, Christopher, 30
Commercials
  rating people's appearance in, 16
Comparable worth, 61–62
Conquistadors
  violence against Native Americans by, 30
Coping with Discrimination (Gabrielle I. Edwards), 61, 64, 66, 68, 80
Coping with prejudice
  legally, 107–108
  personally, 106–107
  politically, 108
Country clubs
  quotas for Jewish membership in, 55–56
"Crafty Oriental", 48
Cuba
  Spanish settlement of, 41
Cuban Americans, 45
Cuban Revolution, 41
Cultural identity
  African Americans, 36–37
  Native American activism and, 33–35
Cultural prejudice, 10–12
  African Americans—*See African Americans*
  blaming the victim, 22–27
  hate groups, 27–28
  myths and stereotypes about, 28–29
  Native Americans—*See Native Americans*
  similarities and differences, 25–29
Custer, General George S., 32
Customs, 10

D

Dade County (Florida), 91
Day care, 62–63
Definition of prejudice, 1
Department of Education, U.S., 68
"Dignity" (organization), 89
Disabled—*See Handicapped*
Disciplining of children, 10–11
Discrimination—*See also specific groups*
  definition, 2
  examples, 2
  explicit, 16–17
  institutionalized, 17–21
  legal, 2–3

racial prejudice and, 22–29,
117–119
subtle, 3
Disease
as weapon against Native
Americans, 31
Dominican Republic
emigration to U.S. from, 41
Spanish settlement of, 41
Douglass, Frederick, 73
"Dragon Lady," 48

E

Economic competition, 12–15
by Asian Americans, 48–49
by Mexican Americans, 42
Economic inequality
for African Americans, 40
for Asian Americans, 50–52
for women, 60–62, 74
Edwards, Gabrielle I., 61, 64, 66,
68, 80
Elderly—See Age discrimination
El Salvador
emigration to U.S. from, 41
Emancipation Proclamation, 35
Employment
age discrimination in, 101
female discrimination in, 62–
63
institutionalized discrimina-
tion in, 18
"Equal pay for equal work," 60–
61
Ethnic labels, 26
Europe
Africa and Asia view of, in
Middle Ages, 7
disciplining of children, 11
European immigrants
Mexican Americans and, 43
Native Americans and, 29–31
Puerto Ricans and, 44
Explicit discrimination, 16–17

F

Family relations
cultural standards, 11–12
"Female" jobs, 61
Feminists—See Women
Ferdinand, King, 7
Fifteenth Amendment, 28
Filipino Americans
economic inequality of, 51
immigration to U.S., 50
Fire departments
institutionalized discrimina-
tion in, 19, 20
Ford, Henry, 55
Fourteenth Amendment, 28
Frank, Barney, 87, 91
Fu Manchu, 48

G

Garment industry
Jews in, 54
Gay-bashing, 22
Gay people—See Homosexuals
"Gentlemen's Agreement"
(1909), 48
Ghost Dance movement, 32

Golden Age (Spain), 7
Gold rush
Chinese emigration to Califor-
nia during, 47
Native Americans in California
and, 31
Gone with the Wind (film), 66
Graduate schools
institutionalized discrimina-
tion in, 19–20
quotas for Jewish enrollment
in, 3, 54–55
Gray Panthers, 104
Great Plains, 31
Guatemala
emigration to U.S. from, 41
Guests
cultural standards for, 12

H

Handicapped, physically
assumptions about, 102
examples of prejudice against,
98–101
resources for, 111–114
sources of prejudice, 94–96
stereotypes about, 97
Harvard University, 54–55
Hate crimes, 21–23
Hate groups, 27–28
Hawaii
Japanese emigration to, 48
Higher education
women in, 68–69
Hispanic Americans
activism and political movements, 45–46
Cubans, 45
history, 41
immigration to U.S., 41
Mexicans, 42–43
Puerto Ricans, 44
stereotypes about, 8, 41–42, 45
variety of, 41–42
History, 7–10
economic competition, 13
Hitler, Adolf, 56
Hmong
emigration to U.S., 50
Homelessness
resources for, 114–115
Homosexuals
in ancient Greece, 9
attacks against, 22, 89–90
awareness test, 79–80
concern with "acting straight,"
77–78, 92–93
controversy surrounding, 76–
78
discrimination against, 88–89
famous personalities, 87
legal rights of, 90–92
resources for, 119
stereotypes and myths about,
78–88
accomplishments, 87
AIDS, 86
appearance and actions, 81–83
child molesters, 80–81
heterosexual experiences, 84–
85
heterosexual marriage, 86–87
masculinity of women, 84

occupations, 83–84
percentage of population, 87–
88
race, 83
"recruitment" by older person,
80
socioeconomic status, 83, 85
superficial relationships, 86
universal condemnation of, 85
violence against, 22, 89–90
Hong Kong
emigration to U.S. from, 49–50
Hosts
cultural standards for, 11–12
Housing
resources for, 115
Howard Beach (New York City
district), 21–22
Hudson, Rock, 82
Hughes, Langston, 87
Human rights
resources for, 110–111

I

Illegal immigration
Hispanic Americans, 41
Immigration Act (1924), 48
Immigration Act (1965), 49
Immigration to U.S.
Asian Americans
postwar immigration, 49–50
before World War II, 47–48
Hispanic Americans, 41
Mexicans, 42–43
Jews, 53–54
India
European view of, in Middle
Ages, 7
Indian Americans
economic inequality of, 52
immigration to U.S., 49–50
Indian languages, 34
Industrialization
women and, 72
Insecurity, 15–16
Institute for Sex Research, 82
Institutionalized discrimination,
17–21
Native Americans and, 33–34
women and, 62–63
Insurance companies
institutionalized discrimina-
tion in, 18
Integration
civil rights movement and, 39
Iranians, 57
Irish
stereotypes and discrimina-
tion against, 8
Iron Range (Minnesota), 13
Isabella, Queen, 7
Islam
homosexuality and, 85, 89
Israel
Arab Americans and, 57
Italians
stereotypes about, 8

J

Japanese Americans
economic success and, 50–51
immigration to U.S., 48

labor market and, 48–49
during World War II, 49
Jews
    American Nazi party, 28
    anti-Semitism, 53–56
    economic advantages of early
        immigrants, 54
    emigration to U.S., 53
    from Germany, 53
    quotas in graduate school for,
        3
    homosexuality and, 85, 89
    legal discrimination, 2
    in medieval Spain, 7
    stereotypes about, 52–54
Jim Crow laws, 37–38
Judaism—*See Jews*
Juries
    women's rights and, 72

K

Kehoe, Alice, 33
Kinsey Report, 87–88
Know Nothing party, 53
Koch, Ed, 91
Korea
    U.S. industry in, 44
Korean Americans
    economic inequality of, 52
    immigration to U.S., 49–50
Ku Klux Klan, 27–28, 37, 38

L

Labor market
    Asian Americans in, 48–49
    women in, 74
La Follette, Robert M., 55
Lakota people, 31, 32
Language discrimination
    voter registration forms, 19
Legal discrimination, 2–3
    Chinese immigration, 47
    Jim Crow laws, 37–38
Legal rights
    coping and, 107–108
    homosexuals and, 90–92
    resources for, 110–111
Lesbians
    stereotypes about, 82, 84
Lewis and Clark, 30
Lithuanians
    stereotypes about, 8
Little Big Horn, Battle of
    (1876), 32
Longtime Companion (film), 85
Lorde, Audre, 85
Los Angeles
    police violence against Afri-
        can Americans in, 21–22
Lowell (Massachusetts), 72

M

Magazine publishers
    intitutionalized discrimination
        by, 19
Male-female behavior
    cultural standards for, 12
"Male" jobs, 61, 69
Marlowe, Christopher, 87
Mead, Margaret, 85
Media
    homosexuals
        bias in, 89

portrayal of, 91
    women
        violence against, 66
Medical profession
    homosexuals
        bias in, 89
Medical schools
    institutionalized discrimina-
        tion in, 20
Mexican Americans, 42–43
Mexico
    emigration to U.S. from, 48
    Spanish settlement of, 41
    U.S. industry in, 44
Migrant farming
    Mexican Americans, 43
Miller, Earl, 61–62
Mining
    Chinese immigration, 47
Minnesota Iron Range, 13
Monthly Labor Review, 61–62
Moors
    religious tolerance of, 7
Mott, Lucretia, 73
Movie studios
    institutionalized discrimina-
        tion in, 19
Muslims
    in medieval Spain, 7

N

National Association for the Ad-
    vancement of Colored People
    (NAACP), 107
National Center for Educational
    Statistics, 68
National Federation of Priests'
    Councils, 89
National Organization for
    Women (NOW), 107–108
Native Americans, 2–3
    activism of, 33–35
    cultural identity, 34–35
    political movements, 33–34
    poverty, 33
    history of, 29–33
        European settlement, 29–31
        institutionalized discrimina-
            tion, 33, 34
        population, 32–33
        reservation system, 32
        treaties with U.S., 31–32
        stereotypes about, 29
Naturalness of prejudice, appar-
    ent, 7–8
Navratilova, Martina, 87
Nee, Victor, 50–51
Neighborhood violence, 21–23
New York City
    anti-Semitism in, 53
    hate crimes in, 21
    political activism among
        Puerto Ricans in, 46
Nicaragua
    emigration to U.S. from, 41
North America
    European settlement of, 29–31
    native peoples attitudes in, 9
North Dakota, 31

O

Obesity
    resources for, 115

O'Connor, Sandra Day, 75
Oral sex, 90
Organizations
    institutionalized discrimina-
        tion in, 17–18
Organized violence, 27–28

P

Paddywagon, 8
Philippines
    emigration to U.S. from, 48
Physical abuse
    resources for, 116
Plato, 87
Pocahontas, 30
Pogroms, 54
Poles
    stereotypes about, 8
Police
    anti-gay violence by, 90
    institutionalized discrimination
        by, 19, 20
    violence against African
        Americans in Los Angeles,
        21–22
Political activism—*See Activism*
Politics
    women in, 74–75
Populist movement, 53
Poverty
    African Americans, 39–40
    Mexican Americans, 42
    Native Americans, 33
    resources for, 114–115
Price, John H., 32
Private social clubs and organiza-
    tions
    institutionalized discrimina-
        tion in, 17–18
Professional schools
    institutionalized discrimina-
        tion in, 19–20
Property values, 13–14
Proust, Marcel, 87
Psychiatric profession
    homosexuals
        bias in, 89
Public Law, 103–105, 107–108
Public schools
    institutionalized discrimina-
        tion in, 17
Publishers
    intitutionalized discrimination
        by, 19
Puerto Ricans, 44
Puerto Rico
    Spanish settlement of, 41
    U.S. policy toward, 44

Q

Quotas
    in graduate schools, 3
    of Jewish Americans, 55–56

R

Race
    homosexuality and, 83
Racial prejudice and discrimina-
    tion
    African Americans—*See Afri-
        can Americans*
    blaming the victim, 22–27
    hate groups, 27–28

myths and stereotypes about, 28–29
Native Americans—*See Native Americans*
resources for, 117–119
Railroads, construction of, 31
    Chinese immigration and, 47
    Native Americans and, 31
Rape, 22, 66–67
Recognizing prejudice, 23–24
Reconstruction, 37
"Recruitment," homosexual, 80
Recurrence of prejudice, 26
Redlining, 18
Rehabilitation Act of 1973, 105
Religion
    African Americans, 36
    homosexuality and, 85, 89, 91
    Native Americans, 34
Religious discrimination
    resources for, 117–118
Reservation system, 32
"Restricted" homes, 2
Rich, Adrienne, 87
Rockford (Illinois) Housing Authority, 61
Roman Empire
    lack of discrimination in, 9
    slavery in, 35
Russians
    stereotypes about, 8

S

Sacajawea, 30
Samoa, 85
Sanders, Jimmy, 50–51
Schools
    blaming the victim in, 26–27
    institutionalized discrimination in, 17, 19–20
    Native Americans and, 34
    quotas for Jewish enrollment in, 54–55
Segregation
    handicapped and, 103
    Jim Crow laws and, 37–38
Seniority
    women and, 63
Sex and sexuality
    age discrimination, 102
    homosexuality, 77
Sex crimes and harassment
    homosexuality and, 80–81
    resources for, 116
    women and, 22, 63–65
Sex discrimination
    resources for, 119
Sexually transmitted diseases
    resources for, 120
Sharecropping
    African Americans, 37
Siberia
    native peoples in, 9
Singer, Isaac, 54
Sioux—*See Lakota*
Slavery, 35–37
Smiling
    in infant girls, 70
Social clubs
    institutionalized discrimination in, 17–18
    quotas on Jewish membership in, 55–56

Socioeconomic status
    homosexuals and, 83, 85
Sodomy, 90
South America
    emigration to U.S. from, 41
South Dakota, 31–33
Southeast Asia
    emigration to U.S. from, 49–50
Southwest U.S.
    political activism among Chicanos in, 46
Spain
    religious tolerance by Moors in, 7
Spanish
    settlement of North America by, 41
    violence against Native Americans by, 30
Spanish-American War, 41
Spicer, Edward A., 33
"Spousal rights"
    for homosexuals, 91–92
Stanton, Elizabeth Cady, 73
Stein, Gertrude, 87
Stereotypes
    Asians, 48–49
    disproving, 4
    generalization from, 5–6
    Hispanic Americans, 41–42, 45
    Irish, 8
    Jews, 53–54
    success of, 52
    property values and, 14
    southern and central Europeans, 8
    teenagers, 4–5
    women, 3–4
Stone, Lucy, 73
Stonewall riots, 90
Straight people
    anti-gay feeling and, 92–93
Stuyvesant, Peter, 53
Supreme Court, U.S.
    backlash against homosexuality in, 90

T

Table manners
    cultural standards, 11
Taiwan
    emigration to U.S. from, 49–50
    U.S. industry in, 44
Teenagers
    insecurity and stereotyping among, 15–16
    stereotypes about, 4–5
Television studios
    institutionalized discrimination in, 19
Tenant farming
    African Americans, 37
Textile mills
    women in, 72
Thais
    emigration to U.S., 50
Thanksgiving, 30
"Thank you"
    cultural standards for, 11
Thirteenth Amendment, 35
Trade unions
    overcoming prejudice through, 13

Treaty of 1868, 31

U

Unemployment
    Native Americans, 33
United Farm Workers (UFW), 46
United Nations
    Lakota people, 32
Universities—*See Colleges*

V

Victims
    Hispanic Americans, 44–45
    stereotypes, 26–27
Victorian era
    pregnancy during, 70
Vietnamese
    emigration to U.S., 50
Violence
    against Arab Americans, 57
    against Asian Americans, 51
    hate crimes, 21–23
    hate groups and, 27–28
    against homosexuals, 89–90
    against Jews, 56
    against women, 65–68
Vote, right to, 2–3
    African Americans, 39, 73
    women, 10, 72–73
Voter registration forms
    institutionalized discrimination in, 19

W

Want ads
    institutionalized discrimination in, 18
West Coast
    Chinese emigration to, 47–48
Whitman, Walt, 87
Wilde, Oscar, 87
Williams, Tennessee, 87
Women
    African Americans, 40
    age discrimination against, 101
    biological factors, 69–71
    career choices, 68–69
    child-rearing, 62–63
    common situations faced by, 58–60
    comparable worth, 61–62
    day care, 62–63
    economic inequality, 60–62, 74
    legal limits on immigration of Chinese, 47
    lesbians, 82, 84
    male-female behavior, 12
    medical schools, 20
    quotas in graduate schools, 3
    resources for, 119
    right to sit on juries, 72
    right to vote, 2, 10, 72–73
    seniority, 62–63
    sexual harassment, 63–65
    sexual violence against, 22
    stereotype of women driver, 3–4
    violence against, 65–68
    working mothers, 9–10
World War II (1939–45)
    Japanese Americans during, 49